Managing
Employee
Absenteeism

Managing Employee Absenteeism

Susan R. Rhodes

SYRACUSE UNIVERSITY

Richard M. Steers

UNIVERSITY OF OREGON

▲▲ **Addison-Wesley Publishing Company**
Reading, Massachusetts • Menlo Park, California • New York
Don Mills, Ontario • Wokingham, England • Amsterdam • Bonn
Sydney • Singapore • Tokyo • Madrid • San Juan

The Addison-Wesley Series on Managing Human Resources
Series Editor: John P. Wanous, *Michigan State University*

HD
5115
·R46
1990

Fairness in Selecting Employees
Second Edition
by Richard D. Arvey and Robert Faley

Managing Conflict at Organizational Interfaces
by L. Dave Brown

Increasing Productivity Through Performance Appraisal
by Gary P. Latham and Kenneth N. Wexley

Managing Careers
by Manuel London and Stephen A. Stumpf

Employee Turnover: Causes, Consequences, and Control
By William H. Mobley

Organizational Entry:
Recruitment, Selection, and Socialization of Newcomers
by John P. Wanous

Library of Congress Cataloging-in-Publication Data

Rhodes, Susan R.
    Managing employee absenteeism / Susan R. Rhodes, Richard M.
Steers. — 1st ed.
        p.   cm.
    Bibliography: p.
    Includes indexes.
    ISBN 0-201-51041-3
    1. Absenteeism (Labor)   2.   Personnel management.   I.   Steers,
Richard M.   II. Title.
HD5115.R46   1990
658.3'14 — dc20

89-14944
CIP

ABCDEFGHIJ–BA–89

*Dedicated
with love
to our daughters,
Kendra, Kelly, and Kathleen,
the managers of the next generation*

Foreword

The publication of *Managing Employee Absenteeism* marks the renewal of the Managing Human Resources Series for the 1990s. As this new decade begins, ambitious plans have been made by Addison-Wesley to revise and expand this series. This book is the first of the new titles. The success of previously published books in this series means that revisions will also be forthcoming.

Managing Employee Absenteeism continues the tradition in this series of meeting two objectives. Each author is asked to produce a book that is state-of-the-art — one that will show academic researchers the cutting edge of a particular human resource topic. At the same time, however, authors are asked to write so that each book can be appreciated by a wider audience of college students and human resource professionals. Both Rhodes and Steers have accomplished these tasks admirably.

Preface

As North American companies increasingly become aware of the new global competition and the concomitant pressures of expanding productivity and efficiency, responsible managers of both large and small companies are turning their attention to discovering ways to improve overall organizational effectiveness. Managers research the merits of off-shore production, increased automation, quality control circles, employee involvement programs, and so forth, all in order to discover ways to deliver a quality product to market at an acceptable price. In this search for competitiveness, a key factor that is often ignored is the actual day-to-day management of a company's existing labor force. That is, managers often focus their attention on what they are doing *to* employees rather than on what they are doing *with* them. In point of fact, employees represent not just one of the largest costs of business, but also one of the largest reservoirs for productivity, if properly managed.

One of the more important factors of managing productivity is employee attendance. Absenteeism costs North American companies tens of billions of dollars each year. While much of this is unavoidable — people become ill — a large percentage of absenteeism is avoidable for companies sufficiently committed to creating an attendance-oriented climate. The question for management is how best to determine and implement an absenteeism policy that is fair both to employees (in accounting for legitimate absences) and to the company. First, it is necessary to clearly understand the primary causes of absenteeism. The informed manager can then develop a program or procedure that fits a company's particular culture and maximizes the probability that employees will want—and be able—to come to work. In this way, the company enhances the likelihood that its human resources are being more fully utilized and that the company is more competitive.

This book is written for all people—managers, researchers, and students—who are genuinely interested in the topic of absenteeism. We shall first examine the extent of the problem, followed by a review of different methods for measuring and costing absence. Next, we review the research literature and a new model of absence behavior that incorporates both voluntary and involuntary attendance. Based on this, we explore different strategies used by corporations to improve attendance at work. Throughout, our goal is to develop a better appreciation for the complexity of the attendance process and for the challenges faced by managers in attempting to address this problem.

In preparing this book, we have been particularly fortunate to have good advice and counsel from several quarters. Our research and theoretical efforts have benefited from the work of several researchers who have made valuable contributions to the field, most notably Professors Paul Goodman of Carnegie-Mellon University, Gary Johns of Concordia University, Canada, and Nigel Nicholson of Sheffield University, England. We also appreciate the helpful review comments of Professor Johns and Series Editor John Wanous of Ohio State University. Considerable help was also provided by the editorial staff of Addison-Wesley, especially Mary Fischer, Loren Hilgenhurst Stevens, Mary Dyer, and Lynne Doran. Our secretary, Pam Hoyle, and graduate assistants, Jeanne Johnstone, and Isabelle Tulaney, were of immense assistance in getting the final manuscript into shape. And, finally, we owe a special note of thanks to our families for their patience and thoughtfulness throughout the process.

Syracuse, New York   S.R.R.
Eugene, Oregon   R.M.S.

Contents

Managing Employee Absenteeism

Absenteeism in the Workplace

1

To many in the world of work, absenteeism is one of those intractable problems for which there is no clear culprit and no easy cure. The "problem" of absenteeism is endemic; it pervades organizations that are public and private, large and small, urban and rural. Moreover, absenteeism as a general phenomenon does not discriminate against individuals on the basis of sex, creed, race, religion, or national origin, although variations can be found across groups for a variety of reasons. And despite efforts to reduce the incidences of absence from work, little in the way of sustained progress has been made. It is truly an issue of central concern to most organizations and managers committed to effective operations, whether they are in the field of government, industry, health care, or education.

Absenteeism is also a topic that often brings quick and definitive responses from administrators and employees alike. We are reminded of a manager who felt so strongly about absent workers that he once stated that his company had no problem with absenteeism but it did have a significant turnover problem because every time employees were absent he fired them! Conversely, we have also heard on numerous occasions about employees who feel that occasional absences from work are part of the psychological contract with one's employer or that they are justified in view of the poor wages or working conditions on the job. However we view it, absenteeism is a subject about which many people have strong feelings.

INITIAL PROPOSITIONS ABOUT ABSENTEEISM

Clearly, we have much to learn about the subject of employee absenteeism. As we shall see, there is considerable disagreement concerning several aspects of the problem (see, for example, Fichman, 1988; Goodman and Atkin, 1984a; Nicholson, 1977). These disagreements include how best to measure absenteeism, what constitute the major causes of absenteeism, and what can be done to reduce such behavior. There is even disagreement as to whether we should even try to reduce it at all. Despite these problems, however, it is fair to acknowledge that there are some points on which most researchers agree. Agreement tends to center on four propositions, which we offer as a starting point for our examination of absence behavior in organizations.

> *Proposition 1:* Absenteeism is pervasive throughout organizations of different types, among different groups of people, and in different countries.

> *Proposition 2:* Absenteeism is expensive for both organizations and individuals.

> *Proposition 3:* Absenteeism is influenced by a constellation of often interrelated factors.

> *Proposition 4:* Absenteeism is associated with a number of important consequences, both positive and negative.

Each of these propositions will be examined here as a prelude to a more detailed analysis of the dynamics of absence behavior at work.

Extent of Absenteeism

To begin with, there is a fairly universal consensus that absenteeism is pervasive across both organizational and international boundaries. For example, within the United States, we can see a fairly consistent pattern of absence behavior across organizations of varying size, in different industries, and in different regions of the country. One of the most rigorous and comprehensive studies of absence rates found that average absenteeism in the United States is about 4.7 percent (Klein, 1986). This includes both voluntary and involuntary reasons and covers all full-time nonfarm employees. Of this rate, it was estimated that 2.6 percent was attributed to illness and accidents, and 2.1 percent was caused by a variety of other reasons.

Before continuing, think for a moment about what would happen to attendance and subsequent productivity if corporate wellness programs could result in even a small reduction in illness-related absenteeism, if better corporate safety measures could slightly reduce accidents, and if better reward and opportunity programs could slightly reduce "voluntary" absenteeism. Even marginal declines in each of these three categories could add up to rather sizeable increments in productive worktime, thereby significantly increasing organizational efficiency and productivity.

If we compare this 4.7-percent absence rate with rates of other industrialized countries, we find that the United States ranks somewhere in the middle *internationally*. Specifically, the Klein (1986) study found the following rates internationally: England (11.8), Canada (11.6), Denmark (7.7), France (5.9), the Netherlands (5.4), Ireland (5.2), Australia (4.3), Belgium (3.8), Greece (3.1), West Germany (3.0), Sweden (3.0), Italy (2.9), and Japan (2.5). It should be remembered here that these are only estimates and that the quality of data and the measurement techniques vary from country to country. For example, another study found Italy to have the highest absence rate in Western Europe (14 percent), not one of the lowest (Yankelovich, 1979). Hence, there is considerable room for error in these comparisons. Moreover, these data say nothing about productivity at work, only presence at work.

Within the United States, differences in absence rates can be identified across industries and occupations, as shown in Table 1.1. For *industries,* it will be noted that average absence rates in the service sector are higher than in the manufacturing sector. Klein attributes this to renewed efforts in manufacturing to reward attendance and punish absenteeism through a "carrot-and-stick" approach (including bonuses for attendance and employee counseling programs), whereas in the service sector far less attention has been given to the problem. Similarly, absence rates tend to be lower in business organizations (for example, 4.4 percent in goods-producing industries) as compared to professional services like hospital workers and teachers (5.8 percent) and to government agencies (5.9 percent). Klein points to the liberal leave policies for federal, state, and local government employees as being responsible for public agencies' having the highest average absence rates.

Differences are also noted across *occupations* as shown in Table 1.2. Executive and managerial positions see a relatively low absence

Table 1.1
U.S. absence rates by industry.

INDUSTRY	ABSENCE RATE (PERCENT)
Goods-producing industries	4.4
Mining	4.0
Construction	4.3
Manufacturing	4.4
Transportation and public utilities	4.8
Wholesale and retail trade	4.7
Finance, insurance, and real estate	4.1
Professional services	5.8
Education	6.2
Health services	5.9
Public administration	5.9

Source: Adapted from B.W. Klein, "Missed Work and Lost Hours, May 1985."
Monthly Labor Review, November 1986, pp. 26–30.

Table 1.2
U.S. absence rates by occupation.

OCCUPATION	ABSENCE RATE (PERCENT)
Executives and managers	4.2
Professional specialists	5.2
Technicians	3.0
Sales representatives	3.9
Secretaries and clerical workers	4.8
Service workers	5.7
Precision production, craft, and repair	4.3
Operators and fabricators	5.5
Machine operators, assemblers, and inspectors	5.3
Transportation workers	4.8
Handlers, equipment cleaners, helpers, and laborers	6.7
Farming, forestry, and fisheries	3.1

Source: Adapted from B.W. Klein, "Missed Work and Lost Hours, May 1985."
Monthly Labor Review, November 1986, pp. 26–30.

rate of 3.2 percent, whereas professional specialists see a much higher 5.2-percent average. Highly-skilled precision production, craft, and repair workers average 4.3 percent, compared to 5.5 percent for the semiskilled group of operators and fabricators. The highest absence

ng unskilled workers, handlers, ers. Clearly, then, industry and o come to work.

FACTORS

nsider *age, gender,* and *union* nage workers consistently have e to the relative importance of :nerally menial nature of their onsibilities. Absences decline 55 years of age. The average for women this average is 6.3 larly high during child-rearing mbers are at least 29 percent members, possibly because of :nce behavior for those under

a with absence is *unemployment* period 1980 to 1985, which in--82, the average absence rate in ercent to 4.7 percent, a 23-per-en unemployment rate and ab-idual, organizational, regional, Aarkham, 1985). Two primary st, employees laid off during

Table 1.3
U.S. absence rates by age and gender (percent).

AGE GROUPS	MALES	FEMALES	TOTAL
All ages	3.7	6.3	4.8
16–19 years	6.7	7.4	7.0
20–24 years	3.9	5.9	4.8
25–54 years	3.4	6.3	4.6
55 years and over	3.0	6.8	5.7

Source: Adapted from B.W. Klein, "Missed Work and Lost Hours, May 1985."
Monthly Labor Review, November 1986, pp. 26–30.

recessions are more likely to be those with high absence rates, and second, remaining employees' fear of job loss will cause greater efforts to attend.

However we look at it, employee absenteeism is extensive. Even so, although we can identify several structural influences, as shown above, we must also recognize that corporations should not rely on crisis management in their efforts to solve the problem. Rather, progress can be made if managers and companies are willing to examine the issue systematically and to initiate creative solutions to the problem.

Costs of Absenteeism

We know that absenteeism can be quite costly. Cost estimates can be calculated in several ways (see Chapter 2). It has been estimated that in the United States alone, absence causes a loss of 400 million workdays per year. Based on this estimate, several researchers have attached a dollar value to this of between $26 and $46 billion per year (Steers and Rhodes, 1978; Goodman and Atkin, 1984a). In Canada, this figure probably approaches $8 to $10 billion. By one estimate, a 1/2 percent change in national absence rates causes a $10 billion change in the U.S. Gross National Product. Hence, however one figures it, absenteeism is an expensive proposition.

Determinants of Absenteeism

Numerous efforts have been made to identify the "key" factors that cause absenteeism. Such efforts usually fail to achieve their objective because they seek simplicity in a complicated organizational world. In fact, a veritable constellation of diverse factors have been found to be related in some fashion to employee attendance. Our own review of the literature (first done in 1977 and again in 1983) revealed 209 such variables (see Table 1.4). Many of these variables were interrelated and overlapping (for example, we identified nineteen job attitudes). Still others were found to be weakly or inconsistently related to attendance or absenteeism. Even so, researchers have thought enough of each one of these variables to examine it in its own right as a possible antecedent (Steers and Rhodes, 1978, 1984).

In fact, the sheer magnitude of the number of antecedents highlights what is perhaps one of the most difficult problems associated

Table 1.4
Number of variables studied in relation to absenteeism.

CLUSTER OF VARIABLES	NUMBER OF VARIABLES IN CLUSTER
Work attitudes	19
Economic and market factors	13
Organizationwide factors	26
Immediate work environment factors	37
Job content factors	30
Personal factors	49
External environmental factors[*]	10
Organizational change[†]	25
Total	209

Source: R.M. Steers and S.R. Rhodes, "Knowledge and Speculation About Absenteeism." In P.S. Goodman and R.S. Atkin (eds.), *Absenteeism: New Approaches to Understanding, Measuring, and Managing Absence.* San Francisco: Jossey-Bass, 1984, p. 234. Reprinted with permission.

[*] External environmental factors are in addition to economic and market factors listed in the table and include temperature, hours of sunshine, geographic region, community support and recognition, and life satisfaction.

[†] Organizational change studies represent those efforts to reduce absenteeism through intervention activities. Variables are in addition to those included in other factors (for example, alcoholism programs, disciplinary programs, health examinations, employee ownership).

with research on employee absenteeism. That is, if such a large number of variables have been found to be associated with absence behavior, can we really draw any meaningful conclusions about principal causes with any degree of certainty? As we shall see in Chapter 3, piecing together the available research findings into a coherent body of knowledge is indeed a challenging task.

Positive and Negative Consequences of Absenteeism

At least two major efforts have been made to examine systematically the extent of the consequences that follow from employee absenteeism. Mowday, Porter, and Steers (1982) pointed out, based on an extensive review, that the consequences of absence can be both positive and negative and can affect the individual, his or her work group, and the organization as a whole. Building upon this work, Goodman and Atkin (1984b; *see also* Goodman and Garber, 1988) extended this analysis and provide an excellent review of the multifaceted consequences of absence behavior (see Table 1.5). Based on available research, these researchers suggested that absenteeism can have consequences (in both a positive and negative way) for up to seven distinct though interrelated groups: the individuals themselves, their coworkers, the larger work group, the organization and its management, the union and its leaders, the family, and, finally, society at large.

Perhaps the most obvious consequences of absenteeism relate to the *individuals* themselves. For individuals, being absent for short periods of time can have several benefits, including temporarily removing oneself from a stressful work environment, allowing time for non-work role obligations (such as taking care of a sick child), allowing time off for a hobby or outside interest (such as fishing), and, in some situations, allowing the individual to comply with workgroup norms "requiring" everyone to take some time off so as not to make other group members look bad. By the same token, however, individual consequences can also be negative as, for example, when absence leads to a loss of pay, disciplinary procedures, or an increased probability of on-the-job accidents when the employee returns to a less-than-familiar job situation. Moreover, it has been suggested that increased absences can also lead to altered job perceptions where individuals feel a need psychologically to justify their behavior (Mowday, Porter, and Steers, 1982; Johns and Nicholson, 1982). Such behavior can cause the individual to distort his or her perceptions of the workplace, thereby distancing the individual from the job.

For the absentee's *coworkers,* absence can oftentimes result in increased job variety and skill development — as well as overtime pay — as they attempt to cover the necessary job functions of those who are not present. Even so, when someone is gone, coworkers can experience an increased workload and increased accidents and conflict levels due to increased stress. Moreover, overtime pay is not always highly prized, especially if it comes at the expense of free time for leisure activities.

For the larger (or extended) *work group,* absenteeism can allow people to learn more jobs, thereby creating greater crew flexibility in meeting production challenges brought on by various reasons. However, these same people can also experience increased coordination problems, decreased productivity, and at times increased accident levels. Hence, for work groups, absenteeism probably has more costs

Table 1.5
Consequences of employee absenteeism.

	POSITIVE	NEGATIVE
Individual	Reduction of job-related stress Meeting of nonwork-role obligations Benefit from compensatory nonwork activities Compliance with norms to be absent	Loss of pay Discipline, formal and informal Increased accidents Altered job perception
Coworkers	Job variety Skill development Overtime pay	Increased work load Undesired overtime Increased accidents Conflict with absent worker
Work group	Crew knowledge of multiple jobs Greater crew flexibility in responding to absenteeism and to production problems	Increased coordination problems Decreased productivity Increased accidents
Organization-management	Greater job knowledge base in work force Greater labor-force flexibility	Decreased productivity Increased costs More grievances Increased accidents
Union-officers	Articulated and strengthened power position Increased solidarity among members	Weakened power position Increased costs in processing grievances
Family	Opportunity to deal with health or illness problems Opportunity to manage marital problems Opportunity to manage child problems Maintenance of spouse's earnings	Less earnings Decline in work reputation Aggravated marriage and child problems
Society	Reduction of job stress and mental health problems Reduction of marital-related problems Participation in community political processes	Loss of productivity

Source: Adapted from P.S. Goodman and R.S. Atkin, "Effects of Absenteeism on Individuals and Organizations." In P.S. Goodman and R.S. Atkin (eds.), *Absenteeism: New Approaches to Understanding, Measuring, and Managing Employee Absence.* San Francisco: Jossey-Bass, 1984, p. 280.

than benefits. The costs and benefits for *management* are similar. Although absenteeism allows management to learn more about the knowledge base of the workforce and often forces companies to provide for greater production flexibility, it also can decrease productivity while increasing costs, accidents, and grievance rates.

For *union officers,* the situation is somewhat different. Moderate absence rates often strengthen the power position of labor leaders, as they are often seen by management as one mechanism to get workers back on the job. Union solidarity also increases at times, especially if union members feel under threat by a management determined to reduce such behavior. At the same time, however, where absence is especially high, union leaders run the risk of losing credibility for being unable to control their own people. Grievance handling costs can also be expected to rise.

Absenteeism has numerous consequences for the *family.* In particular, absence from work allows the employee time to deal with illness or health problems of family members, to help solve marital problems (for example, to spend time with one's spouse), to take care of a problem with one's child (for example, attend a parent-teacher conference), or to "cover" for one's spouse while the spouse makes added income. On the negative side, absenteeism can at times lead to less income for the family, a decline in the work reputation of the family (especially in some cultures like those in Asia), and increased family conflict (for example, where the person absent interferes with the spouse's household routine).

Finally, it can be argued that absenteeism has consequences for *society at large.* Most notably, staying away from a dissatisfying or stressful job can reduce community mental health problems along with their often serious side effects, can reduce various social problems associated with marital relations, and once in a while can even aid in the community political process when, for example, a volunteer city council member misses work to attend an important council meeting. Hence, from a societal standpoint, absences can in some ways result in cost savings ultimately chargeable to taxpayers.

However, absences can also result in increased costs, especially in the form of a general loss in productivity. Productivity losses not only affect corporate profits or organizational efficiency, but in addition ultimately influence GNP and international balance of payments by making one country's products or services less competitive in world markets. This issue applies equally to private and public organizations because both ultimately depend on the efficient utilization of scarce and valued resources to continue operations. As a result, everyone loses when average attendance falls below that of the competition.

PROBLEMS IN THE STUDY OF ABSENTEEISM

On the surface, the study of employee absenteeism should be simple. A person either is or is not at work. However, in actual practice we know that the situation is much more complex. In fact, there are at least two reasons why the study of attendance behavior requires careful attention before attempting to reach any definitive conclusions in a particular organizational situation. First, we often lack clarity concerning the meaning or meanings attached to absence behavior. Absence often means different things to different people. And, second, we need to recognize that there are multiple and often conflicting ways to measure absenteeism. Because of this, it is sometimes difficult to interpret available data on the subject. Let us look at each of these problems briefly.

The Meaning of Absence

Simply put, people often tend to have different perspectives or attach different meanings when viewing the topic of employee absenteeism. Johns and Nicholson (1982, p. 128) highlight this point with the following quote:

> **I** am sometimes prevented from attending work through no fault of my own.
> **You** lack motivation to attend regularly.
> **They** are lazy malingerers, willfully milking the system.

To the manager, absence is often seen as a problem to be solved. Absence is a dysfunctional *category of behavior,* and negative motives are often imputed to the "violator." "Good" employees come to work on a consistent basis; "bad" ones stay away for the slightest reason. Hence, absenteeism becomes a management problem, and good managers solve the problems that confront them. It is a test of effective management.

But to the employee, absence can take on a very different meaning. Absenteeism can be *symbolic* of deeper feelings of hostility or perceptions of inequitable treatment in the job situation. Absenteeism can be a way to "get back at" the organization for a poor work environment, low pay, or other attributes of the job with which employees are dissatisfied. Absenteeism can even be seen by some as a duty to one's coworkers who are also less than perfect in their attendance record; we often feel a need not to make others look bad. Hence, absenteeism can in a very real sense become a *social phenomenon* — as opposed to an individual category of behavior — where the rules of group dynamics apply.

From an administrative standpoint, attempts to understand and deal with absenteeism thus depend upon which implicit theory or assumptions the administrator uses. If the traditional managerial model is employed, resulting action recommendations will more than likely focus on absence control policies. On the other hand, viewing absence more as a social phenomenon may lead the administrator to focus more on improving work attractiveness and developing a culture that facilitates attendance instead of absenteeism. And perhaps a third approach would be to take a somewhat more eclectic stance and recognize that absence is a multifaceted phenomenon, requiring a multidimensional approach to problem-solving. Hence, frame of reference becomes critical when we explore the causes — and possible solutions — associated with absence behavior.

The Measurement of Absence

A second major problem facing those interested in absenteeism is a measurement one. This issue is sufficiently important to warrant special attention in Chapter 2. However, we introduce the issue here simply to highlight its importance to the overall topic of this book. When we talk about absenteeism or look at absence data for a particular organization, it is important to know what is included in the discussion. For example, are we talking about voluntary or involuntary absence? Avoidable or unavoidable? Are these measures combined or separated? And, equally important, exactly how was attendance or absenteeism calculated? As we shall see in Chapter 2, there are several ways to measure this behavior (for example, total number of days absent versus total number of instances of absence regardless of the number of days per instance). The choice of measures depends largely upon what aspect of the issue you wish to focus on. Without an awareness of how the measures were calculated — what is included or not included — any resulting conclusions as to causes or solutions must be suspect.

Clearly, then, as we begin our analysis of absence behavior in work organizations, caution is in order with respect both to the diversity of meanings attached to the behavior and to the way in which it is measured. However we view it, though, we must recognize that employee absenteeism has far-reaching and long-term consequences that affect many people. It is important to understand why people sometimes choose not to come to work when they are fully capable of attending. Moreover, it is important for managers to know when it is necessary to "crack down" on abuse or change the work environment to make it more attractive. But by the same token, it is equally important for managers to understand those circumstances in which people, for whatever reason (illness or otherwise), are genuinely unable to come to work.

In our zeal to "eliminate" absenteeism, we sometimes forget that periodically there are situations when we really don't want people to come to work even when they do (such as the dedicated individual who comes to work with the flu, only to infect those around him or her). We sometimes forget that an occasional "mental health day" can sometimes result in improved, not reduced, long-term performance for an employee. And we even forget at times to apply to ourselves the attendance standards we expect in others. In the analyses that follow throughout this book, it is hoped that a balance can be achieved between seeking ways to reduce unnecessary absenteeism and productivity loss and taking care of the legitimate needs of a company's human resources. Perhaps in the last analysis it is the ability to achieve a workable balance between these seemingly contradictory goals that will determine the ultimate effectiveness of a manager's efforts.

Plan of this Book

In this book, we shall explore the subject of employee absenteeism from several aspects. In this first chapter, we have examined the nature and extent of the "problem." Consideration was given to the costs and consequences of such behavior. In Chapter 2, we will look at measurement issues and see how organizations vary in their assessment methods. Included here will be a discussion of how the costs associated with the problem can be determined. In Chapter 3, efforts to model absenteeism are reviewed and the empirical evidence is examined as it relates to these models. In general, this chapter aims to summarize what we know about the major causes of absenteeism. A general diagnostic model is proposed to guide managerial efforts to understand and deal with absence.

The next three chapters (Chapters 4, 5, and 6) examine various methods used by corporations to reduce absence behavior. These chapters will build upon the diagnostic model presented in Chapter 3. In particular, Chapter 4 reviews absence control policies that have been used with varying degrees of effectiveness on the job. Reward systems and the use of reinforcement techniques are discussed. Chapter 5 then examines what managers can do to enhance or develop an attendance-oriented culture that exhibits a high degree of work attractiveness. Finally, Chapter 6 considers how corporations can improve employees' ability to attend through the introduction of programs relating to physical fitness, child care, and transportation assistance. Throughout, the focus of these three chapters is on helping to improve attendance by making it easier as well as more desirable to come to work.

Concluding comments are offered in Chapter 7 as we consider what might be on the horizon as we continue to seek ways to improve both the quality of the work experience for employees and the effectiveness and efficiency of the organization necessary in an increasingly competitive and demanding environment.

Assessing Employee Absenteeism

2

A survey of 1600 Canadian firms indicated that only 17 percent maintained absenteeism records, despite the fact that 36 percent of these firms considered absenteeism to be among their most severe problems (Robertson and Humphreys, 1978). And in the United States, one study found that 62 percent of the firms surveyed kept records of average absence rates (Prentice-Hall, 1981). In each case, in view of the extent and cost of absence problems to organizations, it is somewhat surprising that such a large proportion of firms do not maintain records.

In this chapter we discuss the measurement aspects of employee absenteeism. We begin by discussing reasons for measuring absence. Following this, methods of gathering absence data are presented. Then we describe a number of indices that can be used to measure absence. Finally, we conclude by discussing how to assess the cost of absence in the organization.

REASONS FOR MEASURING ABSENTEEISM

Measuring absenteeism can serve as many as four purposes for organizations. These include: 1) administering payroll and benefits programs, 2) planning human resource requirements for production scheduling, 3) identifying absenteeism problems, and 4) measuring and controlling personnel costs (Gandz and Mikalachki, 1979).

Administering payroll and benefits programs requires a knowledge of who is present and who is absent from work, as well as the reasons why people are absent. Hence, information for each individual is needed concerning the reason for absence and its duration. In this way the organization can determine whether the absence is compensable under a benefit program or other contractual arrangements.

Planning human resource requirements for production scheduling can be aided by historical data on absenteeism. These data can be used to forecast attendance. In this way, managers can avoid the cost of overstaffing while at the same time protecting themselves against human resource shortfalls.

Answering the question "Does my organization have an absenteeism problem?" obviously entails measuring absenteeism. Because some level of absenteeism is inevitable and unavoidable, the existence of absenteeism does not necessarily indicate a problem. To assess whether there is a problem requires answering questions of comparison: Do certain departments have higher absence rates than other departments within the same organization? How does the organization's absence rate compare with industry, regional, and national absence rates?

And finally, as pointed out in Chapter 1, excessive absence can be costly to the organization. By measuring absence, the organization has the ability to estimate its cost. Moreover, it is possible to determine what proportion of absenteeism can be influenced by managerial action. In this way, policies can be developed and programs can be implemented to control absence behavior.

METHODS OF GATHERING ABSENCE DATA

Methods of monitoring job absence used by 137 personnel executives who were members of the Bureau of National Affairs' *Personnel Policies Forum* are shown in Table 2.1. As shown in the table, in 82 percent of the companies, supervisors are responsible for keeping daily employee attendance records. In 68 percent of the firms a companywide system for collecting and reporting absence data has been implemented. Although variations in record-keeping practices exist between the companies, data are obtained most frequently from time cards or time sheets. Fifty-nine percent of the companies compute

Table 2.1

Recording and measuring job absence, percentage of companies.

	ALL COMPANIES	BY INDUSTRY			BY SIZE	
		Mfg.	Nonmfg.	Nonbus.	Large	Small
Supervisors keep daily employee attendance records	82%	71%	90%	96%	91%	75%
Absence data are collected and reported through a companywide system	68	70	66	64	71	65
Absence rates are computed for at least one employee group on a regular basis	59	72	49	43	55	62
Rates are computed* —						
Monthly	51	63	30	42	50	52
Annually	40	29	55	58	43	38
Quarterly	31	29	40	25	37	28
Weekly	16	27	—	—	7	22
Daily	15	17	10	17	17	14
Other	6	6	10	—	10	4
Absence rates are computed for all regular employees*	57	49	60	83	68	50

Source: *Job Absence and Turnover Control.* Personnel Policies Forum Survey No. 132, p. 3 (October 1981). Copyright 1981 by The Bureau of National Affairs, Inc. Reprinted with Permission.

* Percentages are based on companies that compute absence rates on a regular basis. *Note:* Percentages add to more than 100 percent because of multiple responses.

absence rates for at least one employee group on a regular basis. Of these, 51 percent compute rates monthly and 40 percent annually. Finally, Table 2.1 shows an analysis of survey results by type of industry and size of company.

THE MEASUREMENT OF ABSENTEEISM

Gaudet (1963) early on identified more than 40 indices of absenteeism. More recent work suggests that each measure is composed of two components: 1) the category of absence it represents (Gandz and Mikalachki, 1979) and 2) an absence metric (Atkin and Goodman, 1984). Simply put, absence categories refer to what is measured, and absence metrics refers to how absence is measured.

Absence Categories

Absence categories are typically defined by management based on policies and employer–employee contractual arrangements. One possible categorization system is shown in Table 2.2.

Table 2.2
Absence categories.

Certified medical illness
Certified accident
Work-related accident
Domestic accident
Contractual absence
Jury duty
Bereavement
Union activities
Other
Disciplinary suspensions
Other absences
No reports
Personal or family reasons
Uncertified medical illness or accident

Source: J. Gandz and A. Mikalachki (1979), *Measuring Absenteeism.* Working Paper Series No. 217, University of Western Ontario, p. 11. Reprinted with permission.

Research by Gandz and Mikalachki (1979) demonstrates that the categories in Table 2.2 are conceptually distinct. Correlations between absence categories based on absence data recorded over a twenty-nine-month period in one firm are reported in Table 2.3. The strongest associations existed among those measures in the "other absences" category, that is, no reports, uncertified illness, and personal absences. Suspensions were also associated with no reports, uncertified illness, and personal absences; the reason for this was that the firm gave disciplinary suspensions to employees engaging in these types of absences. However, the associations between certified illness and measures in the "other absences" category were considerably weaker, giving support for the notion that different causal factors are involved.

Absence Metrics

The second component of an absence index is the *metric*. Of the absence metrics, the most commonly used are measures of magnitude, frequency, and duration. In addition to these, Atkin and Goodman (1984) propose four other metrics — measures of return, building, intertemporal lag, and run type — which can be useful in doing research on absenteeism. Each of these will be discussed in turn.

Measures of magnitude

Measures of total time lost per employee during some period of time are categorized as measures of magnitude. Time lost can be measured in hours or days. For example, hours lost per employee would be calculated as follows:

$$\frac{\text{Number of hours absent during time period}}{\text{Total number of employees}}.$$

Such magnitude measures are used by organizations and researchers (Chadwick-Jones, Brown, and Nicholson, 1973; Chadwick-Jones, Nicholson, and Brown, 1982).

Measures of occurrence

Occurrence, or frequency, measures indicate the number of episodes of absence within a particular time period, regardless of their duration. For example, over a one-year time period, if an employee misses a total of ten days from work with three of the days occurring consecutively

Table 2.3
Correlations between days absent for different reasons.

	2	3	4	5	6	7	8
1. Number of reports	0.40**	0.15*	0.22**	0.01	0.37**	0.00	0.22**
2. Uncertified illness		0.26**	0.30**	0.01	0.48**	0.11**	0.32**
3. Certified illness			0.13*	0.03	0.19**	0.05	0.13*
4. Certified accident (domestic)				0.04	0.16**	−0.05	0.18**
5. Certified accident (work)					−0.01	0.03	0.05
6. Personal						0.19**	0.34**
7. Bereavement							0.02
8. Suspension (other)							

Source: J. Gandz and A. Mikalachki (1979), *Measuring Absenteeism*. Working Paper Series No. 217, University of Western Ontario, p. 11A. Reprinted with Permission.

* $p < 0.05$
** $p < 0.001$

due to an illness and the remainder being one-day spells, the frequency of absence would be eight per year.

There are several variants of the occurrence measure. In one instance, a measure was constructed indicating whether an employee was (scored "1") or was not (scored "0") absent during a two-month time period (Newman, 1974). Another variant is to construct a frequency index of short-term absences, including only one- or two-day absence spells (Chadwick-Jones et al., 1982; Terborg et al., 1982).

On the face of it, the calculation of a frequency index appears to be a relatively unambiguous task. However, a number of questions need to be addressed which, if not dealt with, can alter the measurement of this index. As shown in Table 2.4, these questions relate to the definition of an event, the determination of the appropriate time period for measurement, the determination of days to be omitted from the count, and the level of analysis (Atkin and Goodman, 1984).

With regard to the definition of an event, the response to the first question should be that a run of consecutive absences of a single type is *one* event. But what if an employee is absent for six days, the first two days being categorized as sick leave, the second two as annual leave, and the final two as sick leave? Should this be counted as one event or two events of sick leave frequency? Is it a total of three separate events of just one event? Similarly, how do we count runs interrupted by a weekend, holiday, or shutdown? Would this be a single run or two episodes? What about long-term absences (perhaps of four or more days and certified by a medical doctor)? Should they be considered in the frequency index? Researchers who have chosen to exclude long-term absences in the frequency count have done so on the basis that long-term absences reflect involuntary absence, whereas short-term absences are indices of voluntary absence. Although there are no easy answers to these questions, it is important that whatever decision is made it be specified (whether in a research project or by an organization) and that it be consistently followed throughout the organization.

Measures of duration

Duration of absence is generally measured in one of two ways. The first, average length of absences, is measured as follows:

$$\frac{\text{Total days absent}}{\text{Absence frequency}}.$$

Table 2.4
Questions to be addressed in using measures of occurrence.

DEFINITION OF AN EVENT

1. Is a run of consecutive absences of a single type one event or multiple events?

2. Should runs of consecutive absences of different types be considered a single or multiple event?

3. Should runs interrupted by weekend, holiday, shutdown day or strike day be a single run?

4. Should long-term absences be considered at all in the frequency count?

DETERMINATION OF TIME PERIOD

1. What is the rationale for the time period over which frequency counts are conducted?

2. More specifically, has the time period been selected on the basis of theory, or was the time frame chosen to examine the consistency of absence taking?

DETERMINATION OF DAYS TO BE OMITTED FROM COUNT

1. Should frequency counts be adjusted for the number of working days actually possible in a period?

LEVELS OF ANALYSIS

1. What is the appropriate level of analysis — individual, work group, or firm?

Source: Adapted from R.S. Atkin and P.S. Goodman (1984), "Methods of Defining and Measuring Absenteeism." In P.S. Goodman and R.S. Atkin (eds.), *Absenteeism: New Approaches to Understanding, Measuring and Managing Employee Absence. San Francisco: Jossey-Bass, pp. 47–109.*

The second is a measure of percentage of work time lost:

$$\frac{\text{Total days absent}}{\text{Scheduled workdays}}.$$

According to Atkin and Goodman (1984), the problems associated with duration measures are similar to those related to occurrence measures. Table 2.5 delineates some questions that need to be addressed in using duration measures.

Table 2.5
Questions to be addressed in using measures of duration.

DEFINITION OF THE NUMERATOR
1. Are partial days counted as absent days?

DEFINITION OF SCHEDULED WORKDAYS
1. Should work on overtime days and during shutdown periods be included in scheduled workdays?

ISSUES INVOLVING VERY LONG ABSENCES
1. Does the organization reclassify individuals who experience very long absences in ways that confound the data?
2. Is the duration measure distorted by inclusion of a few very long absences?

POSSIBLE EFFECTS OF NATURAL "ANCHORS"
1. Is there an "adhesive effect" exerted by weekends and other natural anchors on the choice of day to return to work after an absence event?

Source: Adapted from R.S. Atkin and P.S. Goodman (1984), "Methods of Defining and Measuring Absenteeism." In P.S. Goodman and R.S. Atkin (eds.), *Absenteeism: New Approaches to Understanding, Measuring and Managing Employee Absence.* San Francisco: Jossey-Bass, pp. 47–109.

Measures of return

Because absence events have distinct beginnings and endings, it would be possible to develop a measure of "return," that is, one that represents when an individual returns to the work situation (Atkin and Goodman, 1984). Such a measure could be based on estimating the conditional probability of not observing an absence on a particular day for an individual, given that the person was absent on a specific number of preceding days. From an organizational perspective, return measures would be useful, for example, when looking at the duration of sick pay and other benefits or when developing or assessing company policy concerning extended absences.

Measures of building

"Building" refers to "extending an unbroken period of absence by the judicious use of a relatively few absence events" (Atkin and Goodman,

1984, p. 76). For example, by taking four absence days between Christmas Day and New Year's Day, when these holidays fall on Fridays, an individual can create a ten-day break from work.

If the practice of building is common within organizations, the consequences can be substantial in terms of lost productivity of those absent as well as in terms of the effect on those present. Moreover, scheduling absence days in a manner that considers organizational needs while being fair to employees can be a challenge.

In spite of its pervasiveness and the possible consequences, the concept of building has been explored only to a limited extent by researchers. The research on building has been principally European in origin and has focused on the "Blue Monday Index" (for example, Behrend, 1959).

Alternative measures of building in the form of the adjacency measure and its variants have been suggested by Atkin and Goodman (1984). The adjacency measure refers to "the number of one-day absences that occur adjacent to a nonwork day, such as weekends, holidays, and known plant shutdowns" (p. 77). One of the variants suggested by Atkin and Goodman is the ratio of adjacent absence days taken to the total possibilities during the work year. This is useful in measuring the frequency of exploiting such opportunities.

Measures of intertemporal lag

These measures and their variants assess the time period occurring between absence events. Such measures can tell us whether there are cyclic aspects to absence at the individual level. Atkin and Goodman suggest four ways of conceptualizing intertemporal lag. First, it can be viewed as a measure of the duration of attendance events. Second, the average observed lag for an individual relative to the expected lag during the course of a given time period can be looked at. Third, lag can be assessed by counting the number of individuals who are not absent during a given time period. (This measure is often used as the basis for attendance reward programs.) Finally, it could be measured as the ratio of average length of absence events to the average length of attendance events.

Measures of run type

Given that absence events can be classified according to type, it is possible that runs of absence events can be comprised of different absence types. For example, several days of sickness might be followed by personal days off, or paid and unpaid absence might comprise a single absence run. The extent of "mixed" runs and the implications of this practice should be more fully explored.

DETERMINING COSTS OF ABSENCE TO THE ORGANIZATION

To determine whether absence is a problem requiring action on the part of the organization, it is important to assess the costs of absence to the organization. In order to do this, time lost to absenteeism must be translated into economic terms. A useful set of decision rules for assessing the costs of absence has been provided by Macy and Mirvis (1976). According to Fig. 2.1, possible costs associated with absence include salaries and fringe benefits of absent workers, productivity loss, overtime costs, replacement personnel costs, additional training costs, and other staffing costs. Table 2.6 shows a step-by-step approach for computing absence costs (Kuzmits, 1979). To demonstrate how to estimate absence costs, we will draw on a hypothetical insurance company, A-One Insurance Company, employing 800 workers as an example. In doing so, each item in the exhibit is explained.

Item 1

Total work hours lost to employee absenteeism for the period should be calculated for *all* employees, including management, professional, clerical and bluecollar. Time lost for all reasons except that sanctioned by the organization (i.e., vacations, holidays, "bad weather" days) should be included. Both whole- and part-day absences should be included in computing the total hours lost. Absences for any of the following reasons would be included in this figure: illnesses, accidents, funerals, jury duty, emergencies, personal time off, and doctor's appointments.

For our example, the records of A-One Insurance show 61,440 total work hours lost to absenteeism during 1987. The rate of absenteeism for this company is 4 percent.

Items 2 and 3

Not all absence is paid time off. For example, some employees might be new-hires who have not accumulated paid sick leave; others might

Figure 2.1
Measuring the costs of absenteeism.

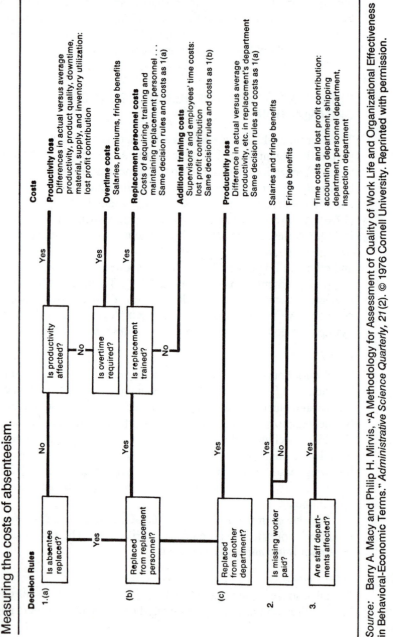

Source: Barry A. Macy and Philip H. Mirvis, "A Methodology for Assessment of Quality of Work Life and Organizational Effectiveness in Behavioral-Economic Terms." *Administrative Science Quarterly, 21* (2). © 1976 Cornell University. Reprinted with permission.

Table 2.6
Estimating the cost of employee absenteeism.

ITEM	
1. Total work hours lost to employee absenteeism for the period:	61,440
2. Total *paid* work hours lost to employee absenteeism for the period:	60,000
3. Total *unpaid* work hours lost to employee absenteeism for the period (Item 1 − Item 2):	1,440
4. Weighted average wage/salary per hour per employee:	$ 9.21
5. Cost of employee benefits per hour per employee:	$ 2.58
6. Total compensation lost to absent employees:	
(a) If absent workers are paid [Item 2 × (Item 4 + Item 5)]:	$707,400
(b) If absent workers are not paid (Item 3 × Item 5):	$ 3,715
(c) Total (Item 6a + Item 6b):	$711,115
7. Total supervisory hours lost on employee absenteeism:	3,333
8. Average hourly supervisory wage, including benefits:	$ 19.20
9. Total supervisory salaries lost to managing problems of absenteeism (Item 7 × Item 8):	$ 63,944
10. All other costs incidental to absenteeism:	
(a) Productivity loss (quantity, quality, downtime, and so on):	$ 00
(b) Overtime costs (salaries, premiums, fringe benefits):	$ 13,800
(c) Replacement costs (costs of acquiring, training, and maintaining replacements):	$ 84,000
(d) Other:	$ 4,000
(e) Total other costs (sum of Items 10a through 10d):	$101,800

(continued)

Table 2.6 (continued)

11. Total estimated cost of absenteeism (Item 6c + Item 9 + Item 10e):	$876,859
12. Total estimated cost of absenteeism per employee [(Total estimated costs)/(Total number of employees)]:	$ 1,096

Source: Adapted from F.E. Kuzmits, "How Much is Absenteeism Costing Your Organization?" *Personal Administrator 24*(6), The American Society for Personnel Administration, Alexandria, VA, pp. 29–33. Reprinted with permission.

use so much sick leave that they exhaust their reserve. Therefore, we must determine how many hours are paid absence and how many are unpaid absence. A-One's payroll records indicate that 60,000 work hours lost were paid (see Item 2) and 1440 were unpaid (see Item 3).

Item 4

The weighted average wage and salary per hour per employee adjusts the average wage of each occupational group by its percent of total absenteeism. For A-One, about 90 percent of all absentees were clerical employees, 8 percent were management and professional, and 2 percent were blue-collar. The weighted average hourly wage rate is calculated as follows:

OCCUPATIONAL GROUP	PERCENT OF TOTAL ABSENTEEISM	AVERAGE HOURLY WAGE	WEIGHTED AVERAGE HOURLY WAGE
Management and professional	0.08	22.00	$1.76
Clerical	0.90	8.00	7.20
Blue-collar	0.02	12.50	0.25
		Total	$9.21

Item 5

The cost of employee benefits per hour per employee at A-One can be estimated by determining the total annual costs of all employee benefits and calculating the percentage of the total payroll costs represented by the benefits. The weighted average hourly wage rate is then multiplied by this percentage to estimate the cost of benefits per hour per employee. At A-One, the cost of benefits is estimated to be about 28 percent of the hourly wage rate, or $2.58 per hour. Included here are organizational contributions to profit sharing, pensions, health and life insurance, and employee vacations.

Item 6

Total compensation lost to absent employees is easily calculated. For paid work hours lost, the weighted average hourly wage figure is included in the calculations. For unpaid work hours lost, hourly benefit costs are simply multiplied by work hours lost.

Item 7

Total supervisory hours lost on employee absenteeism is more difficult to estimate, as the information to do so will not be available in existing records. The basic piece of information needed to estimate this figure is the average number of supervisory hours spent per day dealing with problems created by absenteeism. Such problems might include counseling and disciplining absentees, dealing with production problems, and training and checking on the performance of replacements. To develop this estimate, a representative sample of supervisors can be interviewed. To increase reliability, a semistructured interview approach can be utilized such that each supervisor is asked the same basic set of questions, but probing is used to obtain complete information. In addition to obtaining information on the problems caused by absence and the time spent with dealing with them, the interviewer can probe on variations in time spent depending on temporal fluctuations in absence.

After estimating the average number of hours lost per supervisor per day, the total cost can be determined by multiplying this number by the total number of supervisors and the total number of work days per year. For A-One Insurance, it is estimated that each supervisor spends about twenty minutes per day, or one third of an hour, on absence problems. Assuming that there are forty supervisors who deal with absence problems and that A-One operates 250 days per year, then supervisors invest 3333 hours per year solving problems caused by absent employees.

Items 8 and 9

The average hourly wage plus benefits for supervisors is calculated only for those dealing with absence problems. In the case of A-One, let us assume that the average hourly wage for the forty supervisors is $15.00 per hour and that benefits are $4.20 (28 percent of wages), thus totaling $19.20. Multiplying $19.20 by 3333 hours results in a total of $63,994 in supervisory salaries lost to managing problems of absenteeism.

Item 10

All other costs incidental to absenteeism is a "catchall," so that costs unique to each organization and not included in the previous steps can be identified. As in Item 7, these costs can be difficult to estimate and should be done so based on discussions with managers and supervisors. Such costs can include productivity loss, overtime costs, and replacement costs.

A-One Insurance Company conservatively estimates that other incidental costs total $101,800. In this regard, at least 1000 hours of overtime work are necessary to compensate for absent employees. Using an overtime premium of one and a half times the weighted average hourly rate, overtime costs amount to $13,800 (see Item 10b). In addition, A-One estimates that it is overstaffed by four clerical employees to handle the workload of absent workers. Annual wages, fringe benefits, and recruitment and training costs for these employees total $84,000 (see Item 10c). Finally, for Item 10(d), A-One estimates that approximately $4000 per year in lost sales and policy cancellations result from absence problems.

Items 11 and 12

The total estimated cost of absenteeism is derived by adding Items 6(c), 9 and 10(e). For A-One Insurance, the total is $876,859. Dividing this figure by the total number of employees yields a cost of $1096 per employee per year.

After calculating the costs of absenteeism, the results must be interpreted in a meaningful fashion. Given that absenteeism cost data are not published for industries in the same way that wage surveys, for example, are, there is little in the way of comparative data available for organizations to determine if their costs are out of line with some standard (Cascio, 1987; Kuzmits, 1979). Hence, each organization must establish its own internal standards as to the acceptable level of costs associated with absenteeism.

If it is determined that the costs of absence are severe enough to warrant interventions for the purpose of reducing absence, the cost estimates serve the further purpose of providing baseline data for evaluating the effectiveness of such interventions. To target information, it would be useful to generate cost estimates by units and/or departments in the organization. The success or failure of programs then can be determined based on reductions in absence costs attributed to them.

In summary, measuring employee absenteeism is a critical first step in monitoring and controlling absence. For the absence data to be useful, they must provide relevant information, and they must be collected reliably and accurately. The organization first must assess what absence categories and metrics should be used in order to obtain relevant information. Once this decision is made, a number of questions (see Tables 2.4 and 2.5) need to be addressed to ensure accuracy and consistency in data collection. Finally, measuring absence is important in determining the costs of absence and, consequently, the severity of the absence problem in the organization.

Major Causes of Absenteeism

3

In the previous two chapters, we saw how extensive the problem of absenteeism is. It was pointed out that absenteeism has consequences for the individuals, their coworkers, and the organization. Moreover, it was shown that some of these consequences can be positive, and some are negative. We also explored various ways in which absenteeism could be measured. Based on this discussion, we are now in a position to examine the various way that the subject has been conceptualized or analyzed by major researchers in the field. Hence, the major focus of this chapter is on discovering the major causes of attendance. Based on previous research, a diagnostic model will be presented to help managers more accurately identify factors in their own organizations that influence such behavior. Following this, we will shift attention (in Chapters 4, 5, and 6) to examine various ways in which absenteeism can be reduced. First, however, let us review early approaches to the study of absenteeism as a prelude to model development.

BACKGROUND FOR MODEL DEVELOPMENT

As one reviews the available research on employee absenteeism, one is struck by the general absence, until recently, of any systematic or comprehensive theory development. As Nicholson (1977, p. 232) pointed out, much of the early research focused on "tentative speculations and propositions *ex post facto* to case studies, and a number of more general theories of organizational behavior in which absence is only a minor element." Following Nicholson, these findings and theories can be categorized into three types of explanatory models: 1) *pain-avoidance models,* in which absence behavior is viewed as a flight from negative work experiences; 2) *adjustment-to-work models,* in which absence is seen as resulting largely from employee responses to changes in job conditions leading to a renegotiation of the psychological contract; 3) *decision models,* in which absence behavior is viewed primarily as a rational (or at least quasi-rational) decision to attain valued outcomes. In addition, a final category called "integrated models" can be identified that attempt to go beyond narrow sets of parameters and offer a more complex view of the causes of attendance.

Pain-Avoidance Models

Pain-avoidance models have guided much of absence research over the years (see Hackett and Guion, 1985) and have their origins in the early job satisfaction research. The underlying assumption is that job dis-satisfaction (or negative job attitudes in general) represents the primary cause of absenteeism. Although concluding that there was little empirical evidence for a job satisfaction–performance relationship, Brayfield and Crockett (1955) ventured the opinion that dissatisfied workers would be absent more if their work dissatisfaction was symptomatic of being in a punishing situation. Moreover, Argyle (1972) noted that when work is satisfying people will show up to enjoy it.

Several meta-analyses of the absence–job satisfaction relationship, although presenting somewhat conflicting results, tend to support the conclusion that the pain-avoidance model is overly simplistic (Farrell and Stamm, 1988; Hackett and Guion, 1985; McShane, 1984). McShane's review of twenty-four published studies supported the notion that employees who are dissatisfied with various aspects of their jobs are more likely to be absent. The relationship was strongest for overall and work satisfaction, but coworker, pay, and supervision dissatisfaction also led to higher absenteeism. His results indicated that satisfaction with promotions was the only dimension unrelated to absenteeism. Finally, he found job satisfaction to be more highly related to frequency of absences than to number of days lost.

Farrell and Stamm's (1988) study found significant negative weighted correlations between overall job satisfaction and both total time absent and absence frequency. Finally, Hackett and Guion's meta-analysis results showed that less than 4 percent of the variance in absence measures was explained by overall job satisfaction and its dimensions. Although they did find all corrected mean correlations to be negative, they concluded that the strength of the relationship was very weak. They further argued against third factor variables moderating the job satisfaction–absence relationship in that too much of the variance in correlations reported across studies could be accounted for by statistical artifacts. Although these studies offer slightly different viewpoints on the absence–job satisfaction relationship, none of them reported particularly strong mean correlations.

In addition to the meta-analysis technique, which is based on bi-variate correlations, an examination of multivariate studies of absence in which satisfaction is included as one of the variables is revealing. When considered along with other variables (for example, demographic, prior absenteeism, organizational), work attitudes (including overall job satisfaction, facet satisfaction, organizational commitment, job involvement) generally were not found to be significant predictors of absenteeism. Nonsignificant absence-attitude findings were reported for overall job satisfaction (Breaugh, 1981a; Johns, 1978; Keller, 1983), satisfaction with supervision (Breaugh, 1981a; Johns, 1978; Popp and Belohlav, 1982), and satisfaction with pay, working conditions, coworkers, and equipment (Popp and Belohlav, 1982). In Popp and Belohlav's study, overall satisfaction was a significant predictor of absence frequency but accounted for the smallest amount of variance among the significant variables.

When taken together, the meta-analysis and the multivariate studies provide little support for the "absence as pain-avoidance" theory. Therefore, like Hackett and Guion (1985), we conclude that it is not fruitful to test further any models that are based on the assumption that dissatisfaction is the primary cause of absence. However, sufficient findings are present to warrant the inclusion of attitudinal variables in more comprehensive models of employee absenteeism. Attitudes can at times serve to "pull" the individual toward the organization assuming the attitudes are positive, and the reverse can be expected when attitudes are more negative.

Adjustment-to-Work Models

In adjustment-to-work models, absence from work is viewed as a consequence of organizational socialization and other adaptive processes in response to job demands. Included among adjustment models are the earlier theorizing of Hill and Trist (1953) and Gibson (1966), as well as the more recent models of Rosse and Miller (1984) and Chadwick-Jones et al. (1982).

Hill and Trist's model

Following Hill and Trist (1953), absence is viewed as one of the means of withdrawal from stressful work situations. Other means of withdrawal include turnover and accidents. In the early phase of "induction crisis," turnover is often the preferred mode of withdrawal. During this phase, newcomers typically lack knowledge about absence norms. Unsanctioned absence is the characteristic mode during the middle period of "differential transit." After this, in the "settled connection" phase, the individual substitutes sanctioned absences for unsanctioned absences, and levels of absence are reduced. This model is described as basically one of organizational socialization. That is, in becoming aware of the absence culture of the firm, individuals internalize these norms such that a change in withdrawal behavior consistent with the norms occurs. Accidents become a means of withdrawal if the sanctioned outlets for withdrawal are insufficient.

In providing evidence based on collective trends of accidents and absence to explain individual reactions, Hill and Trist's theory can only be considered to be highly speculative. Not only is there no direct evidence supporting their model, but also it is not clear that testable hypotheses could be developed from it (Chadwick-Jones et al., 1982). Their theory, however, makes a contribution by introducing the concept of social norms of absence.

Gibson's model

Gibson (1966) set forth a comprehensive conceptual model of organizational behavior to explain absence behavior based on the contractual relationship between the individual and the organization. According to Gibson's model, individuals and organizations enter into an exchange relationship in which the individual agrees to contribute his or her competencies in exchange for certain rewards, and the organization agrees to provide rewards for a certain level of effort on the part of the individual. Fundamental to the satisfactory implementation of the contract is the attitude of commitment to both the contract's intent and its terms, or what is termed "authenticity." The more the tasks and rewards of the organization are viewed as satisfying the individual's needs, the stronger will be the individual's identification with and commitment to the organization.

Gibson then applied the model to explain conflicting research in the absence literature. Work identification was viewed as a strong influence on absence behavior, and any factor that served to increase identification operated to reduce absence. Other important influences on absence behavior were the ease of legitimating absences and the perceived authenticity of management. Using his framework, he explained research findings on the relationship between absence and gender, length of service, age, job status, size of organization, and cosmopolitans and locals. Although the research findings he presented appear to be consistent with his theory, they in no way represent a test of his theory. Moreover, as Chadwick-Jones et al. (1982) point out, there is a considerable gap in the level of abstraction of the conceptual model and the methods and data used to support it. Finally, although Gibson provided propositions that were suitable for testing, there have been no following comprehensive tests of his model by absenteeism researchers.

Rosse and Miller's model

More recently Rosse and Miller (1984) focused on the adaptive responses or coping mechanisms available to a worker in coping with his or her work environment. Absence behavior is one of the adaptive responses available to the worker. Because their model was developed in response to the question "What do workers do when they are dissatisfied?" it is concerned with behavioral shifts and is not meant to be a general theory of behavior. According to this view, then, absence behavior would represent a break from normal routine. Although their approach is primarily an adjustment model, it also contains elements of a decision model.

According to Rosse and Miller, a stimulus event (for example, the first warm, sunny day of spring) leads to a state of relative dissatisfaction. This relative state equates with an awareness of a new standard, a negative response (or affect) resulting from not being at the new standard, and an action tendency to achieve the new standard. Next, the individual is viewed as considering behavioral alternatives to achieve the better state. Factors influencing the person's consideration include personal experience, exposure to role models, the presence of clear social norms, and the perception of constraints (that is, ability-induced or environmentally-induced limitations to behavior). The result of this consideration is a set of alternatives, ordered according to the perceived likelihood that they will lead to the person's being better off. The alternative chosen will be the one resulting in the highest positive utility, defined as "the anticipation that the behavior will improve the person's situation" (p. 211).

The environmental responses to the behavior will be experienced by the person as either positive, neutral, or negative. If the consequences are positive, the source of relative dissatisfaction has been eliminated, and successful adaptation has occurred. On the other hand, if the consequences are positive or neutral, the source of relative dissatisfaction is still present, and the individual continues to repeat the adaptation cycle until successful adaptation occurs.

Rosse and Miller's model was examined empirically by a correlational field study designed and carried out prior to the development of the full model (Rosse and Hulin, 1985). As such, the study was not intended to be a formal test, but Rosse and Hulin concluded that the results provided an empirical basis for the model. Their findings indicated that job satisfaction indices were good predictors of intentions to quit, turnover, change attempts, and health symptoms. On the other hand, only satisfaction with work content and coworkers were related to absence behavior. According to Rosse and Miller, however, an adequate test of the model requires a longitudinal within-subject design permitting analysis of work perceptions, decision processes, enacted behavior, and the consequences of that behavior on subsequent cycles. This requires rigorous, labor-intensive studies.

In summary, Rosse and Miller's model makes three useful contributions. First, it focuses on absence as one of several behavioral responses available to individuals in dealing with relative dissatisfaction. This means that it is necessary to consider the relationship between absence and other behaviors. Second, it draws attention to the dynamic nature of absence behavior. Third, in acknowledging that the stimuli leading to relative dissatisfaction can come from within the work environment or outside it, absence behavior as an adaptive response can be viewed within the context of the individual's total life space.

Chadwick-Jones, Nicholson, and Johns's model

The final adjustment model can be distinguished from the other models discussed thus far in that it focuses on the notion of social exchange rather than individual motivations. Moreover, the amount of absences taken is influenced by the prevailing absence culture. This framework was first developed by Chadwick-Jones et al. (1982) and later expanded by Nicholson and Johns (1985).

In viewing absence as part of a social exchange, Chadwick-Jones et al. stress that this is not simply an exchange that occurs between the individual and the organization, as in Gibson's model, but also one that occurs among individuals in the organization. First, the exchange between the individuals and the organization is a "negative exchange" in that the employees are withholding their presence from work, perhaps to make up for workload pressures, stress, or the constraints imposed by fixed work schedules. In some cases, management might tacitly collude with employees in the exchange, for example, in encouraging employees to use up sick days rather than lose them. Second, among employees, absences might be allocated to ensure that workload pressures can be met. Employees might take turns in being absent: "If you were absent last week, then it's all right for me to be absent tomorrow."

Because the absence of one person affects others in the organization, the absence culture sets limits on the appropriate levels of absence. Although interindividual variations in absence do occur, these differences operate within the limits prescribed by the particular culture. Chadwick-Jones et al. (1982, p. 7) define absence culture as "the beliefs and practices influencing the totality of absences—their frequency and duration—as they currently occur within an employee group or organization." Employees are aware, albeit imperfectly, of the nature of this culture. The absence culture then influences the absence norm, which is what employees "collectively recognize (usually with management collusion) as suitable and appropriate for people in the job, their unit, their organization, given the particular conditions, both physical and social, of tasks, pay, status, and discipline" (p. 7).

Following Nicholson and Johns (1985), variations in absence cultures across organizations or groups are predicted to arise from the degree of salience of the culture and the level of trust inherent in the psychological contract (see Fig. 3.1). First, the *salience* of the culture refers to the degree of distinctiveness of beliefs about absence, assumptions underlying employment, and views toward self-control. The more salient the culture, the more homogeneous it is and the more it impacts the individual directly, frequently resulting in clear norms regarding attendance behavior. On the other hand, cultures that are less salient

Figure 3.1
A typology of organizational absence cultures.

		CULTURAL SALIENCE (HORIZONTAL INTEGRATION)	
		Low salience	High salience
PSYCHOLOGICAL CONTRACT	High trust	TYPE I DEPENDENT Deviant absence	TYPE II MORAL Constructive absence
(VERTICAL INTEGRATION)	Low trust	TYPE III FRAGMENTED Calculative absence	TYPE IV CONFLICTUAL Defiant absence

Source: N. Nicholson and G. Johns (1985), "The Absence Culture and the Psychological Contract: Who's in Control of Absence?" *Academy of Management Review 10*, p. 402. Reprinted with permission.

exert more subtle influences on behavior and lead to greater individual variations in absences. Cultural salience is influenced by the organization's absence control system, its technology, and social ecology. Second, the level of *trust* refers to whether the tasks surrounding one's job are high or low in discretion. The four types of absence cultures are: 1) the *dependent* culture (low salience, high trust), characterized by deviant absence; 2) the *moral* culture (high salience, high trust), typified by constructive absence; 3) the *fragmented* culture (low salience, low trust), characterized by calculative absence; and 4) the *conflictual* culture (high salience, low trust) with its resultant defiant absence.

This absence culture framework makes a significant contribution to our understanding of absence behavior in recognizing how constraints can be placed on individual behavior by the collective reality of the organization. Group norms defining what constitutes acceptable behavior must be recognized as an important factor here. However, such an approach can be somewhat limited because it does not give

sufficient attention to individual variations in behavior within an absence culture. That is, there is an equally important need to recognize
individual differences as a factor in absenteeism.

Decision Models

Two primary streams of influence have contributed to the development
of decision models of absence. These are the rational decision models
provided by economists (for example, Allen, 1981; Chelius, 1981;
Gowler, 1969; Winkler, 1980) and sociologists (Adams, 1965) and
the expectancy-valence framework posited by organizational
psychologists (Vroom, 1964; Porter and Lawler, 1968). What these
groups have in common is that they view absence behavior as largely
rational in nature and determined by the individual's subjective evaluation of the costs and benefits associated with absence and its alternative.

Economic models

Economists have drawn on microeconomic theory and labor-
economics analysis. First, Gowler (1969) presented a model of the
labor supply of the firm. According to this model, absence is used by
employees as a way to restore the balance of effort–reward ratios
disturbed by fluctuations in levels of overtime. Second, following
Gowler's lead, Allen, drawing on the concepts of work–leisure tradeoff
and income and substitution effects, developed a model of work attendance. According to his model, absence permits the worker to control
wage levels and other rewards for work when considering desired levels
of work, leisure, and risk. Absence results when the benefits of not
working on any particular day are greater than the costs. Third,
economists have examined the effect of the wage and fringe benefit
structure on absence. For example, we know that when fringe benefits
are not tied to hours worked, an incentive for absence is created
(Deitsch and Dilts, 1981; Dunn and Youngblood, 1986). This is due to
the fact that as work hours decrease, the paid benefits per hour
increase, thus creating an income effect that fosters absence. Supporting the models based on economic theory are studies showing an
increase in absence associated with an increase in the difference
between a worker's marginal rate of substitution of income for leisure
and his or her marginal wage rate (Dunn and Youngblood, 1986),

increased fringe benefits (Allen, 1981; Chelius, 1981), and higher levels of paid sick and absence days (Dalton and Perry, 1981; Winkler, 1980).

Psychological models

Perhaps the most prominent psychological model of decision-making that has been applied to absence behavior is the expectancy-valence theory of employee motivation as developed by Vroom (1964) and extended by Lawler and Porter (1967). This approach integrates decision theory with an analysis of motivational processes. Individuals are regarded as making choices about their behavior based on the probability that they will receive valued outcomes. Although the theory was not originally developed to explain absence, Lawler and Porter argue that it could apply to absence behavior. And although there has not been an empirical test of expectancy-valence theory in relation to absence behavior, the theory has had a pervasive influence on the study of absenteeism (for example, Ilgen and Hollenback, 1977; Morgan and Herman, 1976). Moreover, it had an influence on the development of the original Steers and Rhodes (1978, 1984) model, particularly in explaining the linkage between satisfaction with the job situation and attendance motivation.

Absence behavior is also treated in equity theory (Adams, 1965) as one of the means of restoring equity with regard to the ratio of outcomes received from work and one's inputs in comparison with a relevant other. Absence is a form of leaving the field in order to restore equity. Although notions of equity have been explored in absence research (Dittrich and Carrell, 1979; Patchen, 1960), the ambiguous role of absence in equity theory and the minor role it plays does not make the theory suitable for examining absence behavior.

Finally, integrating psychological and economic approaches to time valuation, Youngblood (1984) viewed absence as a function of motivation processes associated with both work and nonwork domains. First, similar to pain-avoidance models, absence was considered to be a reactive response to an unfavorable work environment. Second, drawing from economic theory, absence was viewed as reflecting proactive behavior for the purpose of restructuring the workweek. Correlational research results provided support for his framework. Youngblood's theory with supporting research suggests the importance of considering the centrality of the nonwork domain in understanding absence rather than simply viewing absence as "organizational" behavior.

INTEGRATED MODELS OF EMPLOYEE ATTENDANCE

In additional to the above three paradigms, two *integrated models* have been developed in an attempt to help explain absence behavior. The first to be published was Nicholson's (1977) attendance motivation model.

Nicholson's Model

The principal assumption underlying Nicholson's attendance motivation model is that attendance behavior is habitual and normal. In searching for causes of absence, therefore, it is necessary to look for factors upsetting the regularity of attendance. Moreover, absence behavior falls on a continuum from unavoidable (A) to avoidable (B). The A–B continuum defines the constraining forces imposed on behavioral choice (see Fig. 3.2). These forces are viewed as varying between individuals and between settings. Absence behavior is triggered by a stimulus or event that affects an individual's needs. The motivational state, or level of attendance motivation, determines whether an event will actually result in absenteeism. Attendance motivation, according to Nicholson, is "largely a matter of the way the need system of the person maps out the properties of work and nonwork environments" (p. 246). Attachment, defined as "the degree to which the employee is dependent upon the regularities of organizational life" and a measurable component of attendance motivation, is the intervening variable influencing absence. Four major sets of influences making up attachment are personality traits, orientation toward work, work involvement, and the employment relationship.

In predicting absence, Nicholson argues that a person with high attachment will not be as influenced by absence-inducing events and consequently will be absent only when events are close to the A side of the continuum. On the other hand, the employee with low attachment will be influenced not to come to work by events not just near the A side but rather all along the A–B continuum.

Nicholson's model makes a valuable contribution to our understanding of absence behavior by providing an integrative framework for examining individual motivation to attend. Moreover, it recognizes the importance of choice in absence behavior and contributes to an understanding of why, when two people are confronted with a similar event (for example, having a cold), one will attend work and the other

Figure 3.2
Nicholson's model of attendance motivation.

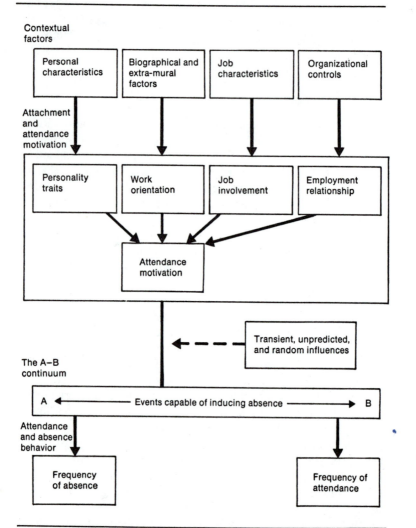

Source: Nigel Nicholson (1977), "Absence Behavior and Attendance Motivation: A Conceptual Synthesis." *Journal of Management Studies, 14*(13), p. 251. Copyright © Basil Blackwell Ltd. Reprinted with permission.

will not. It has been suggested that this model has a shortcoming in that it principally focuses on the work domain (although the concepts could easily be applied to incorporate the nonwork domain) and that the model is difficult to test (as evidenced by the lack of research attention given to it). Even so, this model must be clearly acknowledged as a major influence on contemporary thinking about absence behavior.

Steers and Rhodes's Model

The second integrated model of attendance was suggested by Steers and Rhodes (1978, 1984). This model was developed deductively based on a review of 104 empirical studies of absenteeism. The model represents an attempt to organize the empirical determinants of absenteeism systematically and comprehensively.

Original model

As shown in Fig. 3.3, the original proposed model suggested that an employee's *attendance* (see box 8 in Fig. 3.3) is primarily determined by two important variables: 1) an employee's *motivation to attend* (box 6), and 2) an employee's *ability to attend* (box 7). An employee's motivation to attend, in turn, is influenced by two factors: 1) *satisfaction with the job situation* (box 4), and 2) *pressures to attend* (box 5). The job situation refers to the general work environment, not simply the nature of the required tasks. As such, job situation factors influencing an employee's satisfaction include job scope, job level, role stress, work group size, leader style, coworker relations, and opportunity for advancement. In their review of the literature, Steers and Rhodes (1978) reported that variables largely relating to job content have a stronger influence on actual absenteeism than those relating to job context. Factors acting as pressures to attend work include the economic/market conditions, incentive reward systems, work group norms, personal work ethic, and organizational commitment.

It is important to note that the model emphasizes the joint influence of satisfaction and pressures to attend—not just satisfaction—as they relate to attendance motivation. It would be a mistake to equate job satisfaction with attendance motivation as some have done, because the latter is in fact influenced by a series of factors beyond work attitudes that both "push" and "pull" the employee toward attendance.

As shown in the model, it is also important to recognize a variety of factors that constrain (or at least are believed to constrain) actual

Figure 3.3
Steers and Rhodes's model of employee attendance.

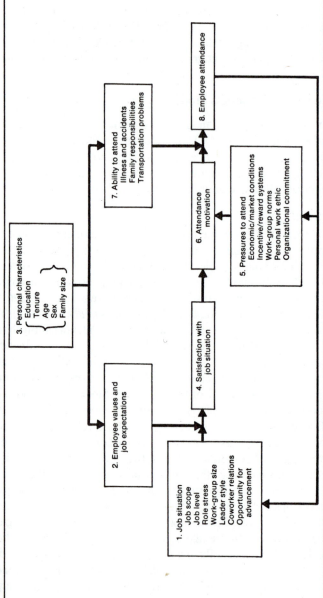

Source: Richard M. Steers and Susan R. Rhodes (1978), "Major Influences on Employee Attendance: A Process Model." *Journal of Applied Psychology*, 63, p. 393. Copyright © 1978 by the American Psychological Association. Reprinted with permission.

attendance. That is, it is not enough simply to be motivated to attend. One must, in addition, have the capacity or *ability to attend*. Factors that can impede ability include family responsibilities (for example, when one's child is suddenly ill), transportation problems (for example, when one's car breaks down), and actual employee illness. (It is ironic that much of the research on absenteeism seems to ignore illness as a leading cause of absence.) Ability to attend thus serves as a gatekeeper, moderating the relationships between attendance motivation and actual behavior.

Research on the Steers and Rhodes model

The model as originally formulated represented an attempt to bring together the disparate and often conflicting findings on the topic found in the research literature. It further attempted to integrate the causes of both voluntary and involuntary absence into one model. In doing so, it was hoped that by providing such a framework, others would be motivated to test all or part of the model. It was recognized, however, that due to the complexity of the model a comprehensive empirical test might not be possible (Steers and Rhodes, 1984). Instead, we would hope to see a series of partial tests that, when taken together, could help researchers better understand the etiology of absence behavior.

Six studies have attempted to test various aspects of the Steers and Rhodes model (Brooke and Price, 1989; Frechette, 1981; Hammer, Landau and Stern, 1981; Lee, 1989; Terborg et al., 1980; Watson, 1981). It is important to note that except for Lee's study, all represent partial tests. Moreover, the timing of the dissemination of results of these studies indicates that most of them were not originally designed for the purpose of testing the model, but rather the Steers and Rhodes framework was applied *post hoc*. The study by Brooke and Price provided a comprehensive test of a modification and extension of the Steers and Rhodes model, but the most comprehensive test of the Steers and Rhodes model in its original formulation was conducted by Lee (1989).

In the first study, Hammer et al. (1981) used the Steers and Rhodes model as a framework for examining patterns of voluntary absenteeism among workers in an employee-owned organization. They examined the influence of job satisfaction, pressures to attend (including organizational commitment and economic commitment), job situation characteristics (including job level and job involvement), individual characteristics (for example, age and education), and union as a mechanism for change on voluntary absenteeism. Using hierarchical regression, they ordered the variables in a sequence of theoretical importance based on the Steers and Rhodes model. That is, job satisfaction, organizational commitment, and financial commitment were entered into the regression in the first three steps because they were identified as the immediate antecedents of withdrawal. These were followed by union as voice, job situation characteristics, and personal characteristics.

Findings indicated that the most important predictors of voluntary absenteeism were pressure to attend work and the belief in the union as a protector of employee rights. Job satisfaction, on the other hand, was not a significant predictor of voluntary absenteeism. Job satisfaction and absenteeism were found to be positively related for employees with high commitment, but no relationship was found for those with low commitment. The effect of interaction between job satisfaction and commitment on absenteeism is not consistent with what would be expected based on the Steers and Rhodes framework. Finally, the importance of pressure-to-attend factors as determinants of absenteeism compared to job and personal characteristics was found to be consistent with the causal ordering of the Steers and Rhodes model.

A second study attempting to provide for a partial test of the model was conducted by Terborg et al. (1980) among a sample of 259 retail employees. This study provided mixed support for the Steers and Rhodes model based on correlational analysis as follows. First, variables indexing ability to attend (that is, family size, gender, job status, and distance from work) were not found to be related to unpaid absence. A problem related to restriction of range of family size and travel distance might have accounted in part for the nonsignificant results. In addition, surrogate rather than direct measures of ability to attend were utilized. Assessing ability to attend more directly might have resulted in stronger relationships.

Second, variables used to capture pressures to attend (that is, organizational commitment, age, and tenure) were found to be significantly related to unpaid absence. The strengths of the relationships, however, were modest. Finally, some support for the model was provided by the results for job satisfaction. Specifically, a weak but consistent negative relationship between satisfaction with work and absenteeism was found. Also, in contrast with past research, pay and coworker satisfaction were negatively related to unpaid absence. Contrary to study hypotheses, overall satisfaction was not significantly related to unpaid absences. Finally, no relationship was found between satisfaction with promotion or satisfaction with supervision and absenteeism.

Caution should be exercised in viewing these results, however, because this study used bivariate correlations to assess model support, whereas the actual Steers and Rhodes model use multivariate determinants. Moreover, although Terborg et al. did perform a number of hierarchical regression analyses to examine the effects of groups of variables on absenteeism, these variables were not categorized according to the major blocks of the original model. For example, organizational commitment, a pressure-to-attend factor in Steers and Rhodes, was included with overall satisfaction and facet satisfaction as relating to satisfaction with the job situation. Thus, although the results of this study are parallel to those of the original model, several differences emerge that preclude a direct test.

In a third study, consistent with the Steers and Rhodes framework, Watson (1981) hypothesized that absenteeism was jointly determined by personal characteristics, job situation, and job satisfaction variables. Based on a sample of 116 production workers and using a time-lost index of absenteeism, overall multiple regression results were significant although not particularly strong. Moreover, job satisfaction was not found to be a major influence on time-lost absence. Findings also supported sex differences in the predictability of absence. Neither pressure to attend nor ability to attend were measured in this study.

In the fourth study, based on eighty-one manufacturing employees, Frechette (1981) examined the influence of personal characteristics, job satisfaction, and salary (as a pressure-to-attend variable) on voluntary and involuntary absences. Company records on reasons for absences were used to assess ability to attend and, consequently, to classify absences as voluntary or involuntary.

Study results showed a significant relationship between the predictor variables and an absence frequency measure. More variance in absence was accounted for by the personal characteristics and the pressure-to-attend variable considered together than by the satisfaction measures. Moreover, the absence model being tested predicted absence frequency better than time-lost absence and predicted both voluntary and involuntary absence.

The fifth study used path analysis based on LISREL estimates to test a modification and extension of the Steers and Rhodes model (Brooke, 1986; Brooke and Price, 1989). In this test, several aspects of the original formulation were changed to improve the ease of testing (see Fig. 3.4). The dependent variable in this study was absence frequency as measured by self-reports. Variables in the model accounted for 21.6 percent of the variance in absenteeism, with significant direct effects being found for 1) the ability-to-attend factors of alcohol involvement and kinship responsibility; 2) overall job satisfaction; 3) pressure-to-attend variables of organizational permissiveness and pay satisfaction; and 4) job situation variables, including role ambiguity and centralization.

The results regarding job satisfaction and absenteeism suggest that, in contrast with Hackett and Guion's (1985) conclusion, it might be premature to discount the role of job attitudes in explaining absence behavior. Determinants of job satisfaction included routinization, work involvement, centralization, and role ambiguity. Variables having the strongest total effects on absenteeism were kinship responsibility, role ambiguity, and organizational permissiveness. Although a direct effect between organizational commitment and absenteeism was hypothesized, it was not supported. Finally, the role of attendance motivation (the key variable mediating between satisfaction with the job situation and pressure-to-attend variables and subsequent absenteeism in the Steers and Rhodes model) was not explored in this study.

The final study, based on a sample of 687 employees of a large financial institution, was the first test of the Steers and Rhodes model to include all major theoretical components (Lee, 1989). The dependent variable was an attendance index representing the number of days at work divided by the number of possible work days, adjusted for vacations and holidays.

For the antecedents to employee attendance, the theorized linkages in the model were empirically supported by a series of regression analyses. First, values, expectations, and ability to attend were each regressed against personal characteristics (for example, tenure, educational level, age, sex, and number of dependents). Sex was the only significant predictor of value congruence, and number of dependents was the only significant predictor of ability to attend. Second, job satisfaction was regressed against 1) expectations, 2) values, 3) the job situation (that is, role stress, leader's structure, leader's consideration, and job level), and 4) interactions between the job situation variables and expectations/values. Results indicated that it was not the job situation per se that influenced job satisfaction, but rather the interaction of the job situation with one's values and expectations. In par-

Figure 3.4
Brooke & Price's model of absenteeism.

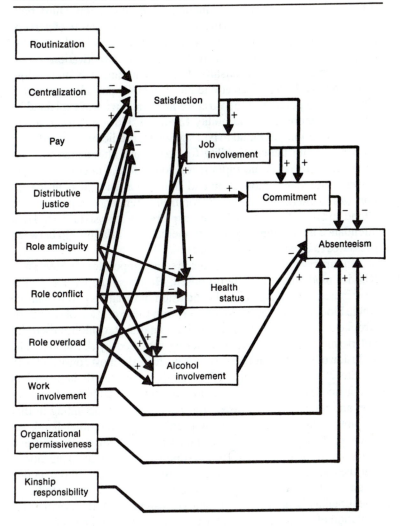

Source: Paul P. Brook (1986), "Beyond the Steers and Rhodes Model of Employee Attendance." *Academy of Management Review, 11,* p. 350. Reprinted with permission.

ticular, the interactions between expectations and stress, expectations and leader's consideration, and values and leader's consideration contributed significantly to the explanation of job satisfaction. Third, both job satisfaction and pressures to attend (that is, a composite of perceptions of labor market conditions, personal work ethic, and organizational commitment) were predictors of attendance motivation.

The theorized relationships between attendance motivation, ability to attend, and actual attendance were only partially supported. First, only 2.5 percent of the variance in attendance was explained by attendance motivation and ability to attend. However, while attendance motivation was found to be a significant predictor of attendance, the relationship between ability to attend and attendance was not supported. Moreover, no support was found for an interaction effect between attendance motivation and ability to attend. Also, little support was found for the feedback loop from attendance to pressures to attend and the job situation. Finally, exploratory analysis indicated that attendance motivation appeared to mediate the relationship between pressures to attend and attendance.

In summary, these studies provide some support for the Steers and Rhodes model as originally proposed. However, the earlier studies were generally incomplete in the inclusion of variables, often omitting whole blocks of the model. Moreover, with the exception of studies by Brooke and Price and by Lee, the data analysis techniques used did not permit testing the causal ordering specified by the model. The inclusion of variables in Lee's study is perhaps the most consistent with the Steers and Rhodes model. This study is particularly important in that it finds support for the relationship between attendance motivation and attendance. However, the results are disappointing in that employee attendance was weakly predicted. On the other hand, explaining 21.6 percent of the variance in absenteeism, Brooke and Price's study provides the strongest support for the utility of the model, but their study tested a modified and extended version of the model. Even so, the general trend of the results of these various studies is encouraging, both in terms of their consistency with the original formulation of the model and in terms of their suggested new directions for research and model development.

New directions for model development
In the realm of scientific research, theories and models are meant to be evolutionary, not static. As one model is tested and as we learn more

about a subject, new formulations emerge that improve our understanding. Our original formulation of an absenteeism model is no exception. When it was first proposed in 1978, the research literature on absenteeism contained scarcely more than one hundred empirical pieces. Now there are more than twice this number and, in addition, the quality of this newer research is significantly better. We have also had several efforts to test various parts of the original model. Based on recent theory and research, it is logical to conclude that perhaps the original model has served its purpose in stimulating thought and investigation on the subject and that now we should turn our attention to asking what modifications might be suggested to improve the overall utility of future models.

As we consider ways to improve model development, some have suggested that the unit of analysis itself should be changed. That is, it has been suggested by some that it is preferable to study withdrawal processes, rather than absenteeism. The argument is advanced that absenteeism, lateness, turnover, and so on, all share similar roots and all influence behavior in similar ways. We disagree with this argument on several grounds (*see also* Clegg, 1983). For example, although Rosse and Miller (1984) assert that absence and other forms of withdrawal "share common roots" and "reliably co-vary," they are talking specifically about the relationship between withdrawal variables and attitudes such as job satisfaction. This approach ignores the multitude of other variables in the equation that clearly have differential impacts on the various withdrawal categories. For example, illness has been shown to influence absenteeism far more than it influences turnover. And absence control policies would be expected to have little influence on turnover. In fact, several writers (for example, Mobley, 1982) have identified a number of reasons that an absence–turnover correlation would not be expected to be high. In view of the uniqueness of absenteeism as opposed to turnover as a category of behavior, it does not appear wise to attempt only to model them within the same framework. This is not to say the two forms of withdrawal are unrelated or that their interrelationships should not be explored. Rather, this is to suggest that if we are to learn more about both behaviors, each might better be served by focusing attention on it as a distinct category of behavior.

If we are to attempt to make improvements in model development, recent research yields several specific suggestions for revision. First, a considerable amount of work has been done recently on the role of work group norms and "absence culture" on attendance (see, for example, Nicholson and Johns, 1985). Of particular interest here is the way in which the salience of good attendance for employees and trust by employees for their managers can be developed. Recent work argues that a culture characterized by high salience and high trust yields higher attendance. This is largely a conceptual argument in the absence of significant empirical support. Even so, there is clearly a need to recognize the social context—a culture that fosters either absence or attendance—more explicitly in absence research. Although the original Steers and Rhodes model does, in fact, recognize work norms as a pressure to attend (see box 5 of Fig. 3.3), in view of recent developments it can be argued that greater emphasis should be placed on this variable.

Second, recent findings indicate that among a constellation of job attitudes, job involvement is often a better predictor of absence than job satisfaction (see, for example, Farrell and Stamm, 1988; Hackett, 1988). At the very least, there seems to be some confusion concerning which attitude is most predictive. In view of this, and in view of the empirical overlap between these and related attitudes (for example, organizational commitment), it might be more useful for purposes of model development to talk in terms of work attitudes in general as an influence on attendance motivation, instead of focusing on one particular attitude, such as job satisfaction.

Third, the original Steers and Rhodes model included "ability to attend" as a factor in actual attendance but failed to make explicit that ability has a perceptual component such that the critical factor becomes the employee's *perceived* ability to attend. Thus, a snowstorm or a bad cold might or might not limit an employee's ability to come to work, depending upon how the employee interprets the situation and its magnitude (see Smith, 1977). What is important is how the individual treats the event and how he or she interprets its impact on ability to attend. As we shall see in Chapter 6, some related work has been done recently that suggests that the role of perceived ability to attend in actual attendance has not received the attention it deserves and that organizations can have more influence on this variable than once thought. Through such recent developments as self-management programs, day-care assistance, employee health management programs, variable work schedules, and car or van pooling, companies can make it easier for employees to attend work. However this is accomplished, preliminary data show that it is possible to increase the likelihood of attendance by removing impediments to employee action.

TOWARD A DIAGNOSTIC MODEL OF ATTENDANCE

Based on the above discussion and the progress that has been made in recent years on the topic, we are now in a position to use this current knowledge to build a diagnostic model of employee attendance. The proposed model is designed to be integrative in that it incorporates new empirical and theoretical developments and because it includes both avoidable and unavoidable absence. Although this model is similar to the original formulation by Steers and Rhodes in focusing on the individual employee's decision to attend, it differs in its increased attention to absence culture, organizational practices, societal context, and perceived ability to attend. These developments follow from recent literature and are included here in an effort to delineate more clearly the major factors influencing such behavior. The model is also meant to be diagnostic in that it is designed to be used not just by researchers but also by managers interested in better understanding the particular forces for absenteeism in their own organizations. In fact, this is the topic of the following three chapters. It is hoped that this model will also continue the research tradition in the field of absenteeism by making use of what we currently know and by challenging others to continue the developmental process.

The *diagnostic model* of employee attendance will be described in three parts: 1) major influences on attendance motivation; 2) major influences on perceived ability to attend and actual attendance; and 3) the role of societal context and reciprocal relationships (see Fig. 3.5). Throughout, it is important to recognize that this is not an organizational or group model of absence; rather, the primary unit of analysis is individual behavior. Thus, the more macro variables are relevant to the extent that they influence individual attendance. In suggesting this paradigm, we recognize that any effort to model complex social behavior can lead to a situation in which some important variables might receive less attention then they deserve. Moreover, causal patterns are often complex or reciprocal, and this point too is sometimes lost or simplified in modeling attempts. Even so, while recognizing the limitations of parsimony, we have attempted in this model to highlight what appear to be the more salient factors that have a fairly significant and consistent influence on absence behavior.

Influences on Attendance Motivation

At least three sets of highly interactive factors can be identified that have an influence on an employee's attendance motivation. These are 1) the prevailing absence culture; 2) organizational policies and practices with respect to the workplace; and 3) employee attitudes, values and goals. Hence, such influences can be found at the individual, group, and organizational levels throughout the organization. Let us see how each of these work.

Absence culture

As discussed earlier in the chapter, the concept of absence culture as originally introduced by Chadwick-Jones et al. (1982) and Johns and Nicholson (1982; see also Nicholson and Johns, 1985) represents one of the signal contributions to the study of employee absence. Absence culture can be defined as "the set of shared understandings about absence legitimacy. . .and the established 'custom and practice' of employee absence behavior and its control" (Johns and Nicholson, 1982, p. 136). Absence cultures can influence attendance motivation and subsequent attendance in at least three ways (Nicholson and Johns, 1985). First, where specific norms exist regarding the appropriate level of absence, an individual's attendance motivation level will often reflect these norms. Second, in the case where no specific norms exist, an individual's behavior can be influenced by his or her observations of the absence behavior of others and the consequences of such behavior. Finally, absence cultures can moderate the relationship between individual values and attitudes and subsequent attendance motivation.

Absence cultures can be distinguished both in their *cultural salience* (that is, the degree to which all members of a group share similar or divergent beliefs about absenteeism) and in their *trust* (that is, the amount of discretion provided employees by their management). High cultural salience means that group members have similar views about what constitutes an acceptable level of absence; low salience means that far less homogeneity exists. It is important to note here that high salience does not imply a norm of low absenteeism; rather, it

Figure 3.5
A diagnostic model of employee attendance.

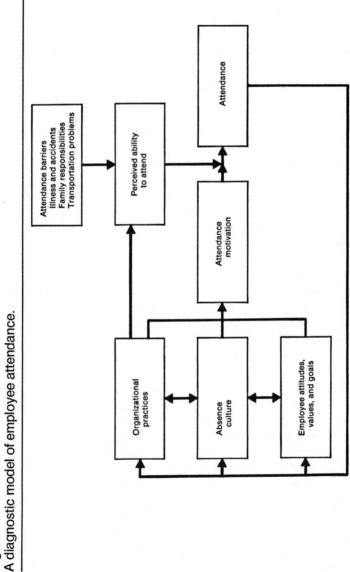

denotes a shared sense of what level or magnitude of absence (high or low) is acceptable.

High trust, on the other hand, occurs when people experience high job discretion (as we see, for example, in professional jobs), leading to a high-trust psychological contract that reinforces the work ethic and internalized commitment to the organization. Low trust results when people experience lower job discretion (for example, assembly line workers) and typically leads to a more detached view of organizational participation and commitment. As noted earlier in the chapter (see Fig. 3.1), these two aspects of absence culture combine to determine which of four "cultures" emerge in an organization (Nicholson and Johns, 1985).

In the final analysis, the nature and quality of these two variables determine the extent to which absence culture influences attendance motivation. For example, when an absence culture is highly salient, it can represent the primary influence on an individual's motivation to attend. On the other hand, when an absence culture is low in salience, other factors (for example, organizational practices or employee attitudes) typically emerge to have a stronger influence on attendance motivation.

Organizational practices

In addition to variations in absence cultures, we must also recognize differences in organizational practices as a major influence on attendance motivation. Such practices can provide either the "push" or the "pull" necessary to encourage attendance. Four such practices can be identified: 1) the nature of an organization's absence control policies; 2) the work design or task interdependencies that characterize a particular job; 3) organizational recruitment and selection practices; and 4) expressed job expectations by management. Although other factors could be added to this list, let us look at these four examples.

First, a company's *absence control policies* represent a particularly salient force for attendance. These policies embody what management thinks constitute acceptable — and unacceptable — levels of absence and reasons for absence. Some companies are noted for their "rigorous" policies and policy enforcement; others are often seen as "lax." Moreover, it is not uncommon to find companies that apply significantly different control policies to managers and nonmanagers; indeed, minimal absence controls are often seen as a fringe benefit for managers. Sometimes these control policies are determined solely by corporate representatives; at other times they follow from contractual negotiations with unions. In any case, they are meant to reflect the basic ground rules governing "acceptable behavior" for whatever group they apply to. (The issue of absence control policies is discussed in detail in Chapter 4.)

Second, the nature of the job itself can influence motivation. Such *work design factors* as work cycle time, role discretion, and task identity, as well as resulting job stressors can often influence how employees see their role in the organization. As noted by Nicholson and Johns (1985, p. 401), "technological and bureaucratic experience may encourage them to see themselves as isolated, dispensable functionaries whose temporary absence is of no fundamental purpose, or they may see themselves as people whose coordinated commitment and reliable attendance is vital to organizational success." Because nonmanagerial positions are more likely to be characterized by low degrees of job discretion, task interdependencies, and perceived importance to the organization, it is not surprising that attendance values at this level tend to be weaker. (The issue of job design as it affects attendance is discussed in Chapter 5.)

A third influence on attendance behavior is the *recruitment and selection practices* of the organization (see Chapter 5). Recruitment and selection practices determine what kinds of people are hired and what kinds are not. To the extent that companies examine job applicants' previous attendance and tardiness records from earlier employment or other pertinent information, it is less likely that absence-prone individuals will actually be hired.

And, finally, to the extent that management communicates *clear job expectations* regarding acceptable levels of absence to both current and prospective employees, we would expect a higher attendance norm. One way to convey such expectations for prospective employees is through the use of realistic job previews (Wanous, 1980), where prospective employees are fully informed concerning job duties and expectations (see Chapter 5). For current employees, such expectations can be transmitted by management through the communication of attendance policies, measuring employee attendance, and performance appraisal and reward practices.

Employee attitudes, values, and goals

Interacting with absence culture and organizational practices in determining attendance motivation is a third critical variable, namely the differences found across employees with respect to their attitudes, values, and goals. These differences can vary considerably from person to person, depending upon what is salient for the individual at a particular point in time. As noted earlier, *work-related attitudes* (for example, job involvement) can play a significant role in determining how employees view the psychological contract between employees and management, as well as how committed they are to coming to work (Farrell and Stamm, 1988; Hackett, 1988). Moreover, attendance motivation can be affected by variations in *personal work ethics,* as well as the *centrality of work* to the employees (that is, how important work is in his or her life goals). In employees who have other interests outside work that take precedence (for example, family responsibilities, hobbies) or to the extent that the work ethic itself is low, we would expect to see a resulting attitude that is conducive to high absenteeism. And, finally, changes in *employee job expectations* (for example, when an employee becomes more "marketable" and begins to reexamine what he or she expects from the job) can influence an employee's view of the importance of coming to work.

Other examples of employee characteristics that can influence attendance can be identified. Whatever the specific set of characteristics, it is important to remember the *interactive* nature between these characteristics and absence culture and organizational practices. For example, variations in work design (for example, a speed-up on the assembly line) or changes in an absence control policy can influence job attitudes. Moreover, a consistently poor work ethic among a group of employees can cause a company to "tighten up" on its absence control policies because the employees might be seen as less trustworthy or committed. And the specificity, consistency of enforcement, and severity of absence control policies can clearly influence cultural salience and the trust dimension of an absence culture. Hence, as shown in Fig. 3.5, these three sets of factors—absence culture; organizational practices; and employee attitudes, values, and goals—interact with each other in a variety of ways ultimately to determine an employee's motivation or desire to come to work.

Influences on Perceived Ability to Attend and Attendance

The second part of the proposed model deals with the link between attendance motivation and actual attendance. As indicated (see Fig. 3.5), attendance motivation leads to actual attendance as constrained by an employee's perceived ability to attend. This perceived ability on the part of the employee, in turn, is influenced by both attendance barriers and organizational practices. At least three attendance barriers can be noted. First, there is the issue of actual *illness or accidents* that physically prevent someone from attending. No responsible company wants sick employees to come to work. Second, *family responsibilities* (for example, a sick child at home) can prevent an otherwise healthy individual from attending. This problem is especially serious for single parents or parents with several children, and the severity of the problem is likely to increase as more young mothers enter the labor force. And, finally, a variety of *transportation problems* (for example, a car breakdown, missing one's bus) can inhibit attendance in spite of one's motivational level.

As will be discussed in Chapter 6, these problems can sometimes be alleviated with the help of the company through such means as company-sponsored day care, car or van pooling, and physical fitness programs. Such organizational practices have become popular solutions in recent years to the problem of how we make it easier for motivated employees to get to work.

As noted in the model, these absence barriers combine with organizational relief efforts and are then assessed by the employee to determine his or her perceived ease of attending. Clearly, the way employees interpret a situation—as opposed to how it "really" is—will influence their actual behavior, and such employees will often see the same situation quite differently. For example, a snowstorm or a car breakdown might cause one employee to yield; whereas another employee might see these events as a challenge to be met. However they see it, the resulting perceptions concerning what is possible or not possible can represent a major influence on subsequent attendance.

Societal Context and Reciprocal Relationships

Finally, it is important to recognize that this sequence of interactive events, although not represented explicitly in Fig. 3.5, is enacted within a particular societal context. Two aspects of this context are particularly relevant to our analysis here. First, general *societal norms* concerning work or the value of work can influence both employee characteristics and organizational practices. Consider the example of work ethics. In Japan, for instance, societal norms stress hard work and the value of being a dedicated employee. It is not surprising, therefore, to find a low average absence rate of one-half percent, compared to almost 5 percent in the United States. Employees in Japan are more committed to coming to work, and companies respond with commensurate and supportive organizational practices. Few control policies are needed because for all practical purposes there is no problem.

Norms can also vary across segments of a larger society, based on such factors as geographic region, occupational grouping, and so forth. For example, occupational groups that are characterized by unionization often feel less commitment to the organization and more to the union, a fact that is capable of influencing absence behavior. Moreover, many companies prefer to open new divisions or plants in rural areas, where it is believed that employee work values and attendance norms are stronger. Finally, norms concerning child-care responsibilities are often different for women and men.

In fact, one could argue that societal norms influence almost all aspects of employee and corporate behavior. Some countries (most notably those in Western Europe) place a high societal value on efficient public transportation systems, thereby alleviating transportation problems for most employees. Moreover, in some societies like Japan, China, and Korea, it is customary for grandparents to assume child-care responsibility for working parents, thus making ability to attend somewhat easier. Thus, the pervasive nature of societal norms and practices should not be overlooked in our efforts better to understand behavior in the workplace.

In addition to societal norms, *economic and labor market conditions* can influence employee characteristics and organizational practices. For example, in periods of tight employment, companies can be reticent to enforce control policies rigorously for valued employees for fear of losing them. Moreover, recruitment and selection practices might not lead to the hiring of "ideal" employees when few job candidates are available. On an individual level, when economic conditions are poor, employees might be more likely to do their best to attend so as not to risk being discharged.

Thus attendance behavior must be viewed within an appropriate societal context. In addition, however, we must recognize several reciprocal relationships that exist within any social dynamic. For example, actual absence behavior is not only influenced by the many variables we have discussed here but also it, in turn, feeds back to influence some of its precursors. High absenteeism within a company, for example, might influence management to tighten its control policies; conversely, high attendance might lead to the opposite effect. High attendance or absenteeism can also influence absence culture, by either reinforcing or challenging the existing culture. Finally, high or low attendance can affect employee attitudes in either positive or negative ways. Hence, the diagnostic model presented here is a dynamic one, where major forces on behavior must be viewed as being in a constant state of flux and where a significant change in one variable can set off a chain reaction that ultimately affects many of the other variables, including attendance behavior itself.

We have now progressed through the available research literature on employee absence. We have seen how model development evolved and we concluded by presenting a new diagnostic model aimed to help both researchers and managers. Based on this presentation, we are now in a position to focus on various remedies to high absenteeism. Hence, in the next three chapters, we will examine various strategies that have proved successful in reducing absence behavior and improving organizational efficiency and effectiveness.

Designing Absence Control Policies

4

We have seen in Chapter 3 that absenteeism is influenced by many causes. Moreover, we have seen that there are several ways in which we can attempt to build a model of the absence process. We turn now to a discussion of what managers and corporations can do to improve actual attendance. Based on the diagnostic model presented in the previous chapter, three rather distinct strategies for absence reduction emerge (see Fig. 3.5). The first general strategy relies on *absence control policies.* That is, it is suggested that managers make use of either positive reinforcement, negative reinforcement, or punishment to shape employees' behavior in the direction of more frequent attendance (or exit from the corporation). Most companies make use of some form of absence control policy. This constitutes the topic for this chapter.

A second strategy that emerges from the model focuses on enhancing attendance motivation by improving the attractiveness of the work environment. Here we are concerned with how managers can improve recruitment and selection techniques to select people more suited for particular jobs, as well as how managers can attempt actually to change the jobs so they are more appealing to more employees. Implicit in this approach are efforts to create a work culture that fosters attendance rather than absence. Hence, we refer to this strategy as developing an *attendance-oriented culture;* we will discuss this in Chapter 5.

Finally, a third approach that can be used in conjunction with the first two involves improving employees' capacity or *ability to attend.* It will be remembered from Chapter 3 that actual attendance is a function of attendance motivation and ability to attend. Hence, whereas Chapters 4 and 5 deal with increasing attendance motivation, Chapter 6 focuses on ability to attend. Taken together, these three strategies are aimed at overcoming most of the barriers to attendance for people, assuming they are physically capable of coming to work.

Let us begin with a discussion of absence control policies. In Italy, a government-owned automobile plant, Alfasud, considers things to be going well when only about 20 percent of its workers fail to come to work (Alfasud, 1979). Under these conditions, car production can reach about 50 percent of plant production capacity. Organizational policies — in particular a counterproductive system of penalties — are seen as the major factors in the high absence rate. For example, if a worker arrives half an hour late to work, he or she is docked part of his salary, whereas if he or she calls in sick there is no penalty. However, for sick leave to be legitimate, it must be for a minimum of three days. Hence, if a worker misses a train connection, he or she is clearly financially better off if he or she returns home and stays home for the next three days than if he or she arrives late for work. As a result, the company loses the services of the worker *and,* in addition, must bear the cost of the first three days of illness — which are not covered by the worker's social insurance.

There is a growing recognition among management and researchers of the role that organizational policies play in encouraging absenteeism rather than attendance (Dalton and Perry, 1981; Winkler, 1980). For example, an increase in sick leave actually taken has been attributed to the implementation of paid sick leave in some but not all cases (Denerley, 1952; Edwards and Scullion, 1979; Sick pay: infectious; 1978; Winkler, 1980; Paringer, 1983). Also, the greater the sick benefits accumulation rate, the higher the absenteeism (Dalton and Perry, 1981). Finally, the policy of not remunerating employees for earned but unused sick leave has been found to be related to absenteeism (Dalton and Perry, 1981).

In this chapter we discuss absence control policies and programs implemented by organizations for the purpose of either controlling sick leave abuse or reducing unscheduled absence. These interventions are designed to increase attendance motivation. Among these techniques are: 1) the use of rewards for good attendance, 2) punishment or discipline for poor attendance, and 3) mixed consequence systems, combining rewards and punishment. First, however, we introduce the the principles of operant conditioning because they provide a theoretical framework for designing effective interventions and procedures for implementation.

PRINCIPLES OF OPERANT CONDITIONING

Operant conditioning is "a *process* in which characteristics of operant or voluntary behavior are, over time, modified by the consequences of that behavior" (Jablonsky and Devries, 1972, p. 341). The underlying assumption of the concept of operant conditioning is that human beings explore, act on, and learn from their environment (Skinner, 1954). Although behavior at first can be random, if a positive consequence follows, the frequency of that behavior will increase. Likewise, if the behavior is not rewarded or is followed by a negative consequence, the frequency of the behavior will tend to decrease.

Four strategies that can be implemented by managers to change the frequency of a behavior such as attendance are: 1) positive reinforcement, 2) negative reinforcement, 3) extinction, and 4) punishment.

Applying a *positive reinforcer* following an operant response strengthens the probability of that response. As was pointed out in Chapter 1, a number of positive consequences for the individual can occur naturally from staying home from work. Positive rewards that have been used to reinforce attendance behavior include monetary rewards, earned time off, and a favorable work schedule (Kempen and Hall, 1977; Reid, Schuh-Wear, and Brannon, 1978; Schmitz and Heneman, 1980).

Negative reinforcement often leads to increased frequency of desired behavior and, hence, is viewed as a positive consequence. In negative reinforcement, an undesirable consequence or aversive stimulus is withdrawn or terminated. For example, increased attendance behavior might result from eliminating the requirement of punching in on a time clock.

The technique of *extinction* refers to withholding a positive consequence, previously administered, for a previously conditioned behavior. Because the behavior is no longer reinforced, it will diminish in frequency and eventually will become extinct. A limitation of extinction is that it does not necessarily lead to the development of the desired response. Moreover, if one has grown to expect a reward, the removal of the reward may be perceived as punishment (Nord, 1969).

A final strategy, and the one most widely used to encourage attendance, is *punishment.* Punishment takes two forms. First, a noxious consequence can be applied for undesired behavior. Second, a positive consequence, not previously connected with the undesired act, can be withheld. A progressive discipline system for continual excessive absenteeism is an example of the former; good attendance being a minimal condition for consideration for promotion is an example of the latter.

Using Positive Reinforcement to Change Behavior

Both the speed with which behavior change occurs and the duration of the effects will be influenced by the timing of the reinforcement. A reinforcement schedule specifies the occurrence of a reinforcer in relation to the behavioral response to be conditioned. The two basic types of schedules having promise for changing employee behavior are continuous and partial reinforcement schedules.

When the consequences occur every time that the response is made, a *continuous reinforcement schedule* is being applied. Continuous reinforcement results in very rapid behavior change. However, when the reinforcer is removed, the behavior decreases rapidly. Because of this and because it is generally impractical for a manager to reinforce employee behavior continuously, it is not recommended for use over long time periods (Hamner, 1974).

A *partial reinforcement schedule,* where a consequence follows only some of the responses, leads to slower learning but longer retention of a response than a continuous schedule. Partial reinforcement can occur on either a ratio or an interval schedule. In a *ratio schedule,* the behavior is reinforced after a specified number of occurrences of the behavior; in an *interval schedule,* the behavior is reinforced after a specified period of time. Both ratio and interval schedules can be either fixed or variable. A *fixed ratio schedule* is one in which a constant number of responses is required for the consequence to occur. Alternatively, in a *variable ratio schedule,* the consequence occurs after a number of desired responses with the number of desired responses changing around an average over reinforcement periods. Hence, an employee working on a ten to one schedule might receive reinforcement after five responses, fifteen responses, eight responses, twelve responses, and so on, to average one in ten. Under the fixed interval schedule, a behavior is reinforced only after a fixed period of time since the last reinforcement. Finally, under the variable interval schedule, reinforcement occurs at some variable period of time around some average.

These four schedules have varying effects upon behavior as follows (Hamner, 1974):

- The *fixed ratio schedule* results in a significantly higher response rate than that obtained under any time-based schedule. The extinction rate, however, is faster than that for variable schedules.

- The *variable ratio schedule* results in more consistent response tendencies than fixed schedules. Moreover, it is the most powerful in sustaining behavior.

- Under the *variable interval schedule,* there will be higher response levels and less fluctuations than under the *fixed interval schedule.*

Using Punishment to Change Behavior

The use of punishment in work settings to change behavior has been criticized by psychologists such as Skinner (1938, 1953) and Bandura (1969) as having harmful side effects and for never fully eliminating undesirable responses. However, a recent review of the literature suggests that available research does not support these criticisms (Arvey and Ivancevich, 1980; Johnston, 1972; Kazdin, 1975; Parke, 1972).

According to Arvey and Ivancevich (1980), the effectiveness of punishment in changing behavior seems to depend on a number of variables as follows:

- *Timing.* Punishment is more effective if applied immediately following the undesirable response than if delayed.

- *Intensity.* Punishment of moderate intensity is more effective than punishment of low or high intensity. Low-intensity punishment might not result in behavioral change, whereas high-intensity punishment might result in such great anxiety that adaptive learning is impeded.

- *Relationship with punishing agents.* Punishment is more effective when the punishing agent has a relatively close and friendly relationship with the punished employee.

- *Schedule of punishment.* Punishment is more effective if it is consistently applied after every undesirable response, if it is administered consistently across different employees by the same agent, and if different agents are consistent in punishing the same undesirable behavior.

- *Provision of rationale.* Punishment is more effective when reasons for the punishment are clearly communicated to the employee and when the employee is informed what consequences will occur for future behavior.

- *Alternative responses available.* Punishment is more effective when alternative desirable responses are available to the employee and these responses are reinforced.

Because of the paucity of research in organizational settings, the above variables are meant to be propositions to guide research and experimentation as contrasted with guidelines for managerial implementation without evaluation.

ATTENDANCE REWARD PROGRAMS

The first major technique for controlling absenteeism relies on reward systems for good attendance. According to a survey of 987 personnel managers sponsored by the American Society of Personnel Administration (ASPA) Foundation (see Table 4.1), organizations use a variety of rewards to reinforce good attendance (Scott and Markham, 1982). Among these are public recognition of good attendance and monetary bonuses for perfect attendance. In addition, some organizations allow employees to accumulate a paid "absence bank," which can be cashed in at a percentage or added to the following year's vacation time. Other rewards reported by respondents in the survey were the perfect/good attendance banquet and the attendance lottery or poker system. It should be pointed out that many of these programs, although utilizing positive reinforcers to reward good attendance, have not been designed with operant conditioning principles in mind. Each of these approaches will be considered separately.

Table 4.1
Rewards used by organizations to reinforce good attendance.

METHOD	PERCENT IN USE	AVERAGE RATED EFFECTIVENESS	ABSENCE RATE: NONUSERS	ABSENCE RATE: USERS
Public recognition of employee good attendance	25%	3.10%	4.6%	3.6%**
Employee bonus for perfect attendance	15	2.96	4.4	4.1
Allow employees to build a paid "absence bank" to be cashed in at a percentage at a later date, or added to next year's vacation time	10	3.28	4.3	4.2
Perfect/good attendance banquet and award ceremony	9	3.19	4.4	3.8*
Attendance lottery or poker system	1	2.77	4.3	4.8*

Source: Dow Scott and Steven Markham, "Absenteeism Control Methods: A Survey of Practices and Results." *Personnel Administrator*, 1982, 27(6), pp. 73–84. Copyright © 1982 The American Society for Personnel Administration, Alexandria, VA. Reprinted with permission.

* Due to greatly imbalanced cell sizes, the difference should not be interpreted.

** Statistically significant $p < 0.05$.

Public Recognition for Good Attendance

As shown in Table 4.1, public recognition for good attendance is the most frequently used reward according to the ASPA Foundation survey. Although the absence rate for users is significantly lower than that for nonusers, users on the average report that this method is only slightly better than marginally effective, with the benefits barely worth the costs.

Contrary to the views of the survey participants, the results of one study suggest that public recognition for good attendance has the potential to be one of the most effective reward programs (Scott, Markham and Robers, 1985). A one-year field experiment involving principally female sewers in six plants compared four approaches to improving work attendance, including financial incentive, recognition, information feedback, and recognition programs with two types of controls. Under the recognition program, employees with no more than two absences were sent a congratulatory card at the end of each quarter. Also, employees missing less than three days of work for the entire year were given a custom-designed piece of jewelry—gold for perfect attendance and silver for one or two days absence. For all four quarters following introduction of the program, significant decreases in absenteeism were found for the personal recognition treatment. On the other hand, the lottery, financial incentive, and information feedback treatments had mixed results with reductions in absenteeism being registered in some but not all of the quarters.

A number of different methods are used by organizations to recognize employees for good attendance records. Among these are publicizing names of these employees in the newspaper, giving the employee a perfect attendance certificate or plaque, sending the employee a congratulatory letter, presenting rewards for attendance at a luncheon or dinner, and displaying an honor roll plaque in the company lobby or other conspicuous place. Public recognition is often used in conjunction with other kinds of rewards.

Employee Bonus for Exemplary Attendance

Monetary rewards for good attendance were given by about 15 percent of the respondents to the ASPA Foundation survey (see Table 4.1). Compared to other types of rewards, this was rated low in effectiveness, being considered slightly less than marginally effective. As will be discussed later in this chapter, perceptions of personnel managers regarding the use of bonuses contradict research findings tending to support its effectiveness.

The design of bonus programs varies considerably according to the requirements that must be met in order to receive a bonus, the nature of the reinforcement schedule employed, and the amount of the reinforcer or reward. In some programs, perfect attendance is required to receive a bonus; in other cases employees receive payment for unused sick days. Weekly, monthly, half-yearly, and yearly reinforcement schedules have been used. Amounts of rewards have varied from $2.50 per week, $50 per semester, or $100 or forty hours' pay for perfect attendance for a six-month period. Annual rewards generally are in the form of either partial payment for unused sick days or an extra week's pay. We shall now take a look at the design and results of some actual bonus reward programs.

School teachers

A school system concerned with the rising costs associated with teacher absence and the difficulty of finding suitable substitutes instituted a program providing a $50 reward for every teacher not absent for an entire semester (Nord, 1970). Any time off, except for attendance at funerals or at court and for at least a quarter of the day, was considered to be an absence. Results of the program were reported for five years of operation. However, no preintervention data were available. The most effective years for the program were the second and third, in which 60 and 54 percent, respectively, of the eligible teachers in the school system had perfect attendance for the first semester. In that the last two years of the program showed a downward trend in attendance toward the first-year level, it appears that this type of reward system is more effective in the short run than the long run. A problem with this study is that no data are given on changes in the overall absence rate.

Production and office workers

An attendance incentive program for 142 nonunion production and office employees provided that employees could either receive $100 or forty hours' pay, whichever was greater, for perfect scheduled attendance over a six-month interval (Grove, 1968). Less than perfect attendance was rewarded by $50 or twenty hours of pay. As a result of this program, the unscheduled absence rate fell from 2.47 percent to 1.53 percent for production employees and from 2.53 percent to 2.13 percent for office employees.

Advertising managers

In yet another program, perfect attenders in a New York-based advertising agency were given an extra week's pay at the end of the year (Prentice-Hall, 1979). Moreover, good attenders were also rewarded with the monetary value of any missed days or hours being deducted from the extra weeks. During the first year of the program, average days lost per employee decreased to 2.4 from 5.8 during the previous year.

Government employees

A program covering 2400 municipal government employees gave employees two rewards (Woska, 1972). First, they received an annual payment of 25 percent of the unused sick leave accumulated over the one-year period. Second, upon termination they were eligible to receive 33⅓ percent of the total accumulated sick-leave credit. In order to be eligible to participate in the plan, employees must have accumulated sixty days of sick leave (taking approximately seven or eight years). Results of this program were highly favorable. Average days per year of sick leave dropped from 6.57 during the year before introduction of the program to 5.84 during the year after its introduction. In addition, sick day usage dropped from 15,391 to 13,987 over the same time period. Finally, the eligibility requirement apparently had some negative effects in that noneligible employees averaged 8.45 days per year sick leave whereas eligible employees lost only 2.27 days on the average.

Part-time janitors

A final program deserves mentioning as it points out the effects of employee participation in program design (Lawler and Hackman, 1969). In this case, nine work groups of part-time employees who cleaned buildings in the evening were involved in a field experiment. Three autonomous work groups designed their own incentive plan to reward perfect job attendance. The conditions of this plan were that employees would receive a bonus of $2.50 per week for each week of perfect attendance. In one group, the bonus was administered weekly;

in two groups, it was dispersed monthly. The company then imposed the plan designed by the three groups on two other groups. The other four groups served as controls: Two groups talked to researchers about attendance problems, but no changes were made in pay plans; two groups received no treatment at all. Only in the case where the work groups participated in plan development did an improvement in attendance occur. For the sixteen weeks prior to the change, the average employee in the participating group attended work for 88 percent of the scheduled hours. After program inception, the attendance rate rose to 94 percent of the scheduled hours.

Later, company management discontinued the incentive plan in two of the three participative groups (Scheflen, Lawler, and Hackman, 1971). In these two groups, attendance dropped below pretreatment levels. In the third group, the rate of attendance remained high. Finally, after one year, attendance improved over pretreatment levels for those groups where the incentive plan had been imposed. For these groups, however, the level of attendance never reached that of the participative groups during the program.

Paid "Absence Bank"

Ten percent of the organizations responding to the ASPA Foundation survey allow employees to accumulate a paid absence bank. As shown in Table 4.1, this method was rated the most effective of the five used to reward attendance. Under this program employees can either add the accumulated hours to next year's vacation or cash in a percentage of the hours in the "absence bank." Hence, this system discourages unscheduled absence while it encourages scheduled absence. We are distinguishing this program as one where extra hours off are accumulated from those discussed earlier in the bonus section where bonuses are paid based on unused leave.

As an example, Pratt and Whitney Aircraft Group at their East Hartford, Connecticut, location gives employees with perfect attendance records for an entire quarter four extra hours of paid time off (Prentice-Hall, 1979). The time off earned can be taken during the year following the year it is earned. To qualify, employees must be present the entire time during each regularly scheduled workday. Except for employees on rotating shifts, vacation days, holidays, and weekends are not counted as scheduled workdays.

Attendance Lottery or Poker System

An infrequently used, yet effective, method for rewarding attendance is the lottery or poker system. The low usage, however, is consistent with the relatively low perceived effectiveness rating given by personnel managers (see Table 4.1). These programs are distinguished from bonus programs in that the timing of the reward is variable as opposed to fixed. According to operant conditioning principles, this results in more consistent attendance behavior, which is sustained over a longer time period. Discussed below are some examples of the mechanics and results of successful lottery and poker system programs.

Hardware store employees

As early as 1966, Leading Hardware, concerned about tardiness and absenteeism among secretaries, sales and stock personnel, and porters, instituted a plan to recognize punctual attendance (Nord, 1970). Each month employees with perfect attendance and punctuality records were eligible to participate in a lottery drawing. One prize for every twenty-five employees was awarded. A drawing for a major award, such as a color TV, was held every six months. Eligibility for this award required perfect attendance and punctuality for the entire six months. Vacation time and funeral leave were the only absences not affecting one's eligibility. This program also included public recognition by printing names of winners and those eligible for prizes in the company newspaper. Results of this program were reported by Nord (1970) after completion of its third six-month cycle. According to personnel department estimates, sick leave payments were reduced 62 percent. Moreover, absenteeism and tardiness decreased during the first year of the program to about one-fourth of their prior level.

Hospital employees

Two financial reward systems involving lotteries were found to be effective in reducing absenteeism among nurses, ward clerks, and nursing assistants in a hospital setting (Stephens and Burroughs, 1978). Under the first system, employees were eligible to participate in a cash prize drawing of $20 only if they had no absences during a three-week period. Under the second system, as long as employees were present at work on eight dates randomly selected from the three-week period, they were eligible to participate in the drawing. As a result of the interventions, absence declined significantly in both groups, from 4.84 to 3.57 percent and from 4.19 to 2.65 percent, respectively. It was expected that the first system would be less effective in reducing absence in that if an individual were absent during the contingency period, the incentive to avoid additional absences would be removed because of the need for perfect attendance. However, no significant differences resulted between the two systems. A final result was a reduction in the percentage of employees experiencing absence from 40 percent before the intervention to 30 percent during the intervention period.

In contrast to the lottery system, in the poker system, employees are given a playing card each day when they arrive at work (Pedalino and Gamboa, 1974; Tjersland, 1972). At the end of the week, the person with the highest poker hand wins a cash award. In one firm the cash award amounted to $20 for the highest hand in each department (Pedalino and Gamboa, 1974). This firm posted cards and hands of each employee on the bulletin board. The unscheduled absence rate decreased from 3.01 percent during the 32 weeks before the poker hand intervention to 2.46 percent during the plan, a reduction of 18.27 percent. Moreover, over the same time period, the absenteeism rate of four comparison groups increased 13.79 percent. Finally, stretching the reinforcement schedule such that the program was operational every other week did not increase the rate of absenteeism over that of the weekly reinforcement schedule.

Overall Effectiveness of Attendance Reward Programs

In the preceding section, we have provided a number of examples of "successful" attendance reward programs, some of which specifically incorporated operant conditioning principles. No attempt was made, however, to assess these programs in a rigorous fashion in terms of their effectiveness in reducing absenteeism. Consequently, a major question that needs to be addressed at this point is: "Are positive reinforcement programs effective in reducing absenteeism?" In answering this question, we first briefly review findings of positive reinforcement studies and then draw on Schmitz and Heneman's (1980) analysis of positive reinforcement programs.

Schmitz and Heneman's (1980) review identified ten studies, all of which reported reductions in absenteeism following the implementation of positive reinforcement programs. Reinforcers found to be effective included bonuses (Grove, 1968; Lawler and Hackman, 1969; Orpen, 1978; Panyan and McGregor, 1976; Scheflen, Lawler, and

Hackman, 1971), bonus points (Baum and Menefee, 1979), participation in lottery (Stephens and Burroughs, 1978; Wallin and Johnson, 1976), participation in poker hand (Pedalino and Gamboa, 1974), and food credit (Kent, Malott, and Greening, 1977).

In addition to the studies identified by Schmitz and Heneman (1980), thirteen other studies have reported positive reinforcement interventions. Reinforcers resulting in reduced absence included reimbursement for unused sick leave, conversion of unused sick leave to vacation leave, a desirable work schedule, feedback and social reinforcement, participation in a lottery, bonus pay, a system involving a choice of rewards, and earned supervisor-scheduled leave (Durand, 1983; Miller, 1978; Reid et al., 1978; Robertson, Johnson, and Bethke, 1980; Robins and Lloyd, 1983; Schlotzhauer and Rosse, 1985; Scott et al., 1985; Silva, Duncan, and Doudna, 1981; Woska, 1972). On the other hand, the introduction of bonus pay, participation in a weekly bingo game, earned time off, a lottery program, and an information feedback program did not lead to reductions in absence (Carlson and Hill, 1982; Gardner, 1970; Scott et al., 1985; Schneller and Kopelman, 1983).

In addition to examining the general effects of positive reinforcement programs, several studies analyzed whether interventions had differential impacts on certain subgroups. In particular, both Stephens and Burroughs (1978) and Schneller and Kopelman (1983) found that there was no relationship between income level of subjects and changes in absence as a result of the intervention. Moreover, previous absence rates and marital status of employees had no bearing on the impact of the bonus program described by Schneller and Kopelman.

Outcomes other than absenteeism were assessed in several studies (Carlson and Hill, 1982; Durand, 1983; Silva et al., 1981). First, improved communication and work attitudes are reported by Carlson and Hill as resulting from a gaming intervention. Here, a weekly gathering to conduct the gaming program was also used as a means of communicating news to employees. Second, the reduction in unscheduled leave resulting from an incentive program among employees in an institution for the retarded led to a general reduction in resident disruptive behavior (Durand, 1983). Finally, negative consequences may occur as a result of an improvement in attendance; Silva et al. (1981) found that as attendance improved, there was a decrease in mean worker efficiency. These results suggest the importance of taking an ecobehavioral perspective, such that consequences, perhaps unintended, other than absenteeism are looked at in assessing the effectiveness of positive reinforcement interventions (Durand, 1983).

All but five of the twenty-two studies reported a reduction in absenteeism following implementation of the positive reinforcement programs. According to Schmitz and Heneman (1980), however, there is reason for both optimism and caution in interpreting the results of these studies.

Reasons for optimism

Due to several factors related to the programs or organizational settings, the results of these studies may actually *understate* the potential effectiveness of positive reinforcement programs in reducing absence. These factors are discussed below.

To begin with, the base-line period absence rates seemed somewhat low in most studies (for example, Grove, 1968; Pedalino and Gamboa, 1974; Robins and Lloyd, 1983; Stephens and Burroughs, 1978). These low rates might have limited the extent to which decreases were possible (a "floor" effect). Therefore, larger reductions in absence rates might occur with higher base-line rates.

Second, in a large number of the studies all absences—voluntary and involuntary—were included in the base-line measure. It might be expected, however, that positive reinforcement programs would have a greater impact on voluntary absences than on total absences. The results, therefore, would underestimate the effect of the program on voluntary absences.

Finally, the monetary reinforcers were, for the most part, relatively small. For example, school teachers received a $50 bonus per semester for perfect attendance. For organizations with paid sick leave programs (a point not generally clarified in the studies), it would seem that the reward would hardly offset the sick leave benefit. It is possible that with larger rewards, even greater declines in absence might occur.

Reasons for caution

For a number of reasons, caution is in order in interpreting results. First, it seems plausible that failures are not so likely as successes to be reported in the literature. Therefore, a positive bias might be reflected in the studies reviewed above. (However, countering this concern, Frederiksen and Lovett (1980), reporting the results of a survey of professionals working in applied settings about their views regarding the status of organizational behavior management, point out that un-published applications were for the most part (90 percent) described as successful.)

Second, the absence of control groups (for example, Panyan and McGregor, 1976; Stephens and Burroughs, 1978; Woska, 1972) and the inclusion of components in addition to positive reinforcement in a number of interventions compromise the internal validity of the studies. Consequently, it is difficult to attribute results to the use of positive reinforcement. In most programs, the intended reinforcer was a monetary bonus; however, such additional features as feedback to employees, unconscious and conscious goal setting, and heightened supervisory attention to attendance problems along with verbal praise might have contributed to reductions in absence, either alone or in conjunction with the bonus.

Third, due to the relatively short time period of data collection while the intervention was in effect, little information is known as to the long-term consequences of the rewards (see Schlotzhauer and Rosse, 1985, for an exception). In addition, researchers rarely ex-amined whether there was a tendency for absence levels to drift higher over time.

A final problem of the studies was the lack of cost–benefit analyses, certainly an important indicator of program effectiveness. Moreover, when these analyses were performed, typically, only direct costs, such as the cost of the bonuses, were assessed. Not provided were costs associated with developing, implementing, and monitoring the pro-gram. In addition, other consequences of the program, intended or unintended, and positive or negative, often have not been evaluated.

To summarize, even though there is relatively consistent support for the association between positive reinforcement programs and reduced absence, questions of causality, long-term effectiveness, and cost effectiveness need to be addressed. Future research should incor-porate rigorous experimental designs including well-matched control groups and pre- and post-intervention time periods suitable for ex-amining long-term effects. In order that changes in both level and trend of absence might be assessed, methods of data analysis, such as time-series analysis (see Glass, Willson, and Gottman, 1975), should be utilized. To eliminate the possibility of a "floor effect," research set-tings should be ones with high voluntary absenteeism. There is a need to evaluate the differential effects of various program components, including the size of monetary reinforcers, the use of other reinforcers (for example, earned time off, favorable schedules), the types of reinforcement schedules, the frequency of reinforcement, the influence of feedback and goal setting processes, and employee participation in program design. Although there is some evidence that responses to reinforcement programs are not influenced by income level (Schneller and Kopelman, 1983; Stephens and Burroughs, 1978), further research on individual differences (for example, age, gender) in responses would be useful in targeting programs. Also, it would be helpful to know whether the programs have a differential effect on those who are chronically absent versus moderate absentees or good attenders. Finally, further evidence of the cost effectiveness of such programs is desirable. To explore this, we are recommending the use of a "behavioral ecology" approach (Durand, 1983). In this regard, it would be helpful to identify not only other consequences of the intervention but also consequences of the change in absence (see Chapter 1 and Goodman and Atkin, 1984b, for a discussion of these).

PUNISHMENT AND NEGATIVE REINFORCEMENT PROGRAMS

The second general approach to absence control policies involves the use of punishment and negative reinforcement. As shown in Table 4.2, a wide variety of punishment methods are used by organizations in an attempt to control absenteeism. In comparing Tables 4.1 and 4.2, it becomes evident that not only are *more* punishment methods used, but they are on the whole used *more frequently* than rewards. Moreover, they are generally viewed as being more effective in controlling absenteeism than rewards. Methods of punishment used by organizations include requiring employees to call in to give notice of absence, progressive discipline and termination for excessive absenteeism, identification and discipline of employees abusing attendance policies, requiring a written doctor's excuse for illness and accidents, interviewing employees after absence, and checking up on absent employees by either a phone call or a home visit. In addition, 43 percent of the organizations reported that they encourage negative peer pressure by requiring coworkers to carry the workload of absent workers. A method used by less than one percent of the organizations (and for good reason, we think) is sending a letter to a spouse pointing out the earnings an employee lost due to absenteeism. The one negative

Table 4.2
Punishment and negative reinforcement methods used by organizations.

METHOD	PERCENT IN USE	AVERAGE RATED EFFECTIVENESS	ABSENCE RATE: NONUSERS	ABSENCE RATE: USERS
Employee call-in to give notice of absence	99%	3.35	7.3%	4.3%*
Termination based on excessive absenteeism	96	3.47	4.4	4.3
Progressive discipline for excessive absenteeism	91	3.43	4.8	4.3*
Identification and discipline of employees abusing attendance policies	88	3.39	4.8	4.3
Require written doctor's excuse for illness/accidents	77	3.05	4.0	4.4
Wiping clean a problem employee's record by subsequent good attendance	47	3.14	4.3	4.3
Peer pressure encouraged by requiring peers to fill in for absent employee	43	2.62	4.3	4.4
Employee interviewed after an absence	35	3.26	4.4	4.2
Spot visitation (or phone call) to check up at employee residence by doctor/nurse/ detective/other employee	21	3.00	4.3	4.3
Letter to spouse indicating lost earnings of employee due to absenteeism	<1	2.50	4.4	1.8*

Source: Dow Scott and Steve Markham, "Absenteeism Control Methods: A Survey of Practices and Results," *Personnel Administrator*, 1982, 27(6), pp. 73–84. Copyright © 1982 The American Society for Personnel Administration, Alexandria, VA. Reprinted with permission.

* Due to greatly imbalanced cell sizes this difference should not be interpreted.

reinforcer included in Table 4.2 is the practice of wiping clean a problem employee's record on the basis of subsequent good attendance.

Employee Call-In

Requiring employees to call in to give notice of absence is used most frequently by the organizations in the survey. According to one correlational research study, this policy appears to be most effective when the employee is required to report in directly to his or her supervisor rather than to a clerk in the office (Winkler, 1980). Hence, the practice reported and recommended by Prentice-Hall (1979) of installing a telephone answering device to aid telephone call-ins may also unwittingly encourage nonattendance.

A field experiment conducted by Ford (1981) demonstrated that it is not employee call-in per se but rather who the employee contacts and the nature of the contact that is critical to reduce absenteeism. In this case a facility for the mentally retarded implemented a policy requiring employees to call their immediate supervisors to give notice of absence. When called, the supervisor questioned the employee about the nature of the illness, whether the employee planned to see a doctor, the name of the doctor, and when the employee expected to return to work. In addition the supervisor informed the employee of the effect of the absence in terms of how many employees were absent due to planned leaves and the number of staffers remaining to do the scheduled work. This procedure replaced one in which employees were required to call in to a central absence-control person rather than to their supervisors.

Using an experimental design, Ford and his associates gathered data under the old system, after which the new system was then implemented for five months. Next, there was a two-month return to the old policy, and finally, the experimental system was reinstituted. Sick-leave hours reported per week decreased from 102.83 hours under the old policy to 97.1 hours when the new policy was first instituted. Surprisingly, when the old policy was reinstituted, sick leave continued dropping to 56.55 hours per week. A return to the "call-your-supervisor" policy resulted in a further decline in the absence rate to 49.75 hours per week. At the same time that sick leave hours declined, there was an increase in vacation time usage per week. Hence, the policy led to employees substituting scheduled absence for unscheduled absence. Finally, it should be pointed out that the fact that absence rates did not return to their old level when the new policy was withdrawn places some doubt on whether the call-in procedure or some other factor might have been responsible for the reduction in absences. It is possible, however, that the procedure led to the development of new norms regarding attendance behavior, which were resistant to change during the short two-month time during which the new policy was withdrawn.

Progressive Discipline and Termination

Progressive discipline and termination for excessive absenteeism were reported to be in use by 96 and 91 percent of the organizations, respectively. These two procedures were rated second and third in effectiveness of the thirty-four control methods in the survey.

In spite of the high regard in which these procedures are held by personnel managers, there are very few examples of instances where progressive discipline and termination have been implemented exclusively with successful results. A discussion of some "unsuccessful" implementations, however, might be edifying.

In a case reported by Nicholson (1976), management concern about an average annual time-lost absence rate of 13 percent among female hourly-paid employees in a food processing plant led to the implementation of a progressive discipline system. This system included a systematic check on absence records along with the issuance of verbal warnings to employees with more than five absence spells (absence frequency) in the previous fifteen months. Next, written warnings were given when absence spells exceeded five in fifteen months. The final step was dismissal, with eight employees being terminated as a result of the program. Before and after results showed a change in the *form* of absence taken, such that employees substituted longer spells for shorter spells and certificated for uncertificated absence. However, there was no overall reduction in the absence rate. Even though one of the goals of the program was to reduce the overall absence rate, this goal was not taken into consideration in designing the punishment system.

Frequently, suspension for excessive absenteeism can be a step in a progressive discipline system. In at least one organization that the authors are aware of, the progressive discipline system including suspension does not work as it is intended. In this particular unionized setting, the first step in the system is that the employee is counseled by his or her supervisor. Then, if attendance does not improve, a letter of warning is given to the employee. This letter offers assistance to the employee, informs the employee that he or she may file a grievance, and states future consequences for continued poor performance. The next step is suspension from work from one to three weeks without pay. Generally, advance notice is given with reasons for the action. Frequently, when employees appeal suspensions by filing a grievance for absence problems they are able to win their cases and receive pay reinstatement for some or all of the suspension period. Hence, what is meant to be a punishment turns out to be a reward as employees receive a "paid vacation" for excessive absenteeism.

Requiring a Written Doctor's Excuse

About 77 percent of the organizations responding to the ASPA Foundation survey reported that they required a written doctor's excuse as a method to control absenteeism. This method was rated to be marginally effective, with the benefits sometimes being barely worth the costs.

A successful implementation of this procedure was instituted by Southern Bell-Georgia (Woodsides, 1980). Under this program, employees were required to have their physicians file a report directly to the medical department of the company for all illnesses over seven days' duration. The role of the medical department was to monitor sickness disability by maintaining contact with the employee, the supervisor, the treating physician, and the benefit department. The monitoring system was intended to reduce sick leave abuse and provide a more accurate determination of expected return-to-work date. During the first year of the program, there was a reduction of $237,000 in total sick leave expenditures along with a downward trend in sickness disability cost per employee.

Wiping Clean a Problem Employee's Record

Removing absence discipline records from the employee's file as a reward for subsequent good attendance is practiced by 47 percent of the respondents to the ASPA Foundation survey. However, it is not clear how effective this method is for encouraging future attendance in view of the results of one study. In this study, Gary (1971) examined the absence records of three categories of employees: 1) those disciplined progressively where the discipline remained a part of their permanent record; 2) those who had been disciplined but not consistently according to the normal progression and/or who later had the discipline removed from their record; and 3) those eligible for discipline based on their records but who never received it. Under the progressive discipline system, the first step was a written reprimand with subsequent suspension and dismissal from work. Results indicated lower casual absences among the first group and higher absences among the second, and even higher absences among the group receiving no discipline. Because the second group includes inconsistent discipline as well as discipline removals, it is with some caution that we suggest that discipline removals might actually tend to serve as rewards for undesirable behavior as opposed to encouraging desirable behavior.

Multiple Consequence Punishment Systems

In actuality, discipline systems instituted by organizations usually involve a variety of punishments, for example, employee call-in, supervisory counseling, progressive discipline, and termination. Below, we describe a successful implementation of an absenteeism control policy incorporating multiple negative consequences.

A six-step procedure for controlling unauthorized absences was implemented in one department of a large manufacturing organization (Baum, 1978). As part of the intervention workers were informed of the discipline procedure for unauthorized absenteeism. Under the procedure, the workers' supervisor maintained detailed attendance records, and workers were required to submit written excuses from legitimate outside sources for unauthorized absences, with questionable excuses being independently investigated. In addition, all workers with unauthorized absences were personally counseled by management. Moreover, excessive absenteeism was penalized by the existing progressive discipline system. Finally, the organization maintained updated discipline and attendance records on all workers. Two comparable departments served as controls. In these departments the existing attendance policy delegating control to the immediate supervisor continued in effect. Under this policy, supervisors had considerable discretion in dealing with absentees; that is, the supervisors made the initial decision as to what action, if any, would be taken for unauthorized absenteeism.

The attendance control policy was particularly effective for chronically absent workers, who were absent on the average 23 days less during the one-year period of the intervention over the preceding year. This reduction in absence was significantly greater than that for their counterparts in the comparison group. On the other hand, the policy did not lead to improvements in attendance among regular attenders. In contrast to Nicholson's (1976) findings that workers substituted certified for uncertified absences to avoid negative consequences of the sanctions, the attendance control policy had no noticeable effect on either long-term illnesses or contractual absences.

Overall Effectiveness of Punishment

In examining how effective punishment has been as a means to control absenteeism, two questions need to be addressed. First, what support is provided by existing organizational research regarding its effectiveness? Second, what influence do arbitral standards relating to just cause have on moderating the effects of punishment, in particular termination for excessive absenteeism, in unionized settings?

Despite the ubiquity of the use of discipline to control absenteeism, there is little research evidence to support its effectiveness. In fact, we could identify only seven studies in work settings which examined the use of discipline alone as a control method. In these studies, control methods have included the discipline interview (Buzzard and Liddell, 1958), employee call-in (Ford, 1981), progressive discipline system and termination (Nicholson, 1976), direct medical reporting (Woodsides, 1980), orientation and counseling (Rosen and Turner, 1971), and multiple consequences (Baum, 1978; Seatter, 1961). Six of the studies reported that the particular intervention was effective in reducing absenteeism. However, in general, the studies were even less rigorous in design than the earlier discussed attendance reward programs. One of the more rigorous studies (Baum, 1978) found that the control policy was effective in reducing absenteeism of chronically absent workers but not of good attenders. As in the case of positive reinforcement programs, we conclude that questions of causality, long-term effectiveness, and cost-effectiveness need to be addressed in future research. Moreover, research is needed on the influence of the design of the punishment intervention on its effectiveness. As discussed earlier, variables that need to be studied are timing, intensity, schedules of punishment, the provision of rationale, and employee's relationship with punishing agent.

In unionized settings with formal grievance procedures, disputes over discipline may be submitted to arbitration. Arbitrators who find that discipline has been administered without just cause may modify the discipline. In such cases, workers terminated for excessive absenteeism may be reinstated. Clearly, this action influences the effectiveness of the punishment meted out by the organization.

Two recent analyses of absentee discharge cases taken to arbitration for the most part reached similar conclusions regarding the factors influencing the arbitral decision (Rosenthal, 1979; Scott and Taylor, 1983). Where the findings of the two studies differ, we can place greater credence in Scott and Taylor over Rosenthal because their review covers 146 cases over a six-year period as opposed to 29 cases over a one-year period.

The question of reasonableness of rules is the threshold question in just cause for discipline (Rosenthal, 1979). Any time a rule is unilaterally imposed by employers, it might be challenged by unions on the basis that it is not reasonable. The criteria used by arbitrators to judge reasonableness generally are inconsistent and subjective. For example, requiring a doctor's statement for illness absence was found to be unreasonable by one arbitrator. On the other hand, a company rule specifying that a doctor's statement would not prevent an absence from being counted in an employee's record was also found to be unreasonable.

Although a rule on its face might be reasonable, its application might be challenged by arbitrators as being unreasonable. According to Scott and Taylor, excessive absenteeism was found by arbitrators to be just cause for discharge in more than half the cases involving this reason. For the most part, where discharge was not upheld by arbitrators, the companies had not correctly set up their policy. Both Rosenthal and Scott and Taylor concluded that arbitrators upheld discharging employees for absenteeism for just cause when the employer adhered to its own rules and consistently applied and clearly communicated its rules. A factor reported by Rosenthal but not Scott and Taylor was maintaining accurate records documenting absence behavior. According to Scott and Taylor, an impartial investigation conducted by employers into the reasons for absence was strongly associated with upholding the discharge. Finally, an improvement factor (for example, wiping an employee's record clean for subsequent good attendance) was not related to case outcome (Scott and Taylor, 1983).

The use of a progressive discipline system was not strongly related to arbitrators' final decisions (Scott and Taylor, 1983). In fact, having a progressive discipline system was significantly related to case outcome only when the case was upheld, but not for denied or split-decision cases. According to Rosenthal, even with a progressive discipline system, arbitrators reinstate employees, despite the severity of the absence abuse, if the rules have not been either fully applied or consistently applied across employees.

MIXED CONSEQUENCE SYSTEMS

The third and final approach to controlling absenteeism combines the use of positive reinforcement and punishment and is referred to as a "mixed consequence system." Four variations have been reported in the literature, including a progressive discipline system with non-monetary privileges for good attendance, a no-fault policy, a leave bank, and a well-pay program.

Progressive Discipline System with Nonmonetary Privileges for Good Attendance

Kempen and Hall (1977) report on two variations of an attendance management system, both of which resulted in decreases in absenteeism. We describe one of these here. This intervention provided nonmonetary privileges to reinforce good and improving attendance along with progressive disciplinary warnings for excessive and worsening absenteeism. If an employee exceeded either seven days absent in the current year or forty days in the current plus previous three years, progressive steps of discipline, that is, a series of warnings, were administered for each new absence occasion. Reinforcement for good or improving attendance included: 1) employees not absent for a thirteen-week period, or having less than two absences for twenty-six weeks, or less than three absences for fifty-two weeks were not required to punch the time clock; 2) employees could earn up to two free unpaid days off per year based on good or perfect attendance; and 3) employees with twenty-one days or less absence over the past three years were awarded disciplinary immunity for a one-year period beginning January 1.

This system replaced a combined punishment and negative reinforcement system. The punishment system consisted of four steps of progressive discipline ranging from informal discussion to consideration for termination. Under the negative reinforcement system, employees could move down the "disciplinary ladder" based on perfect attendance for a twenty-six-week period.

Absenteeism decreased from an average of 6.2 percent during the thirty-four-month baseline period to 4 percent after implementation of the attendance management system. Confounding the results, however, was the fact that a series of layoffs occurred during the experimental period. Even so, analysis indicated that the lowered absence rates could not be attributed to the "survivor" phenomenon. Finally, absenteeism did not decrease significantly during the study period in a comparison group of salaried employees at the plant and hourly employees at eleven equivalent plants.

No-Fault Policy

The no-fault policy described by Kuzmits (1981) is in essence a point-system control policy. Under this system, employees received one point for each absence occurrence regardless of duration and partial points for tardiness and part absences. In addition, employees failing to report their absence by a designated time received two points per infraction. An employee was rewarded by removal of one point for accumulating a perfect attendance record for one month. Disciplinary action was taken based on the accumulated number of points within a twelve-month period. Data gathered for one year prior to and one year following introduction of the system indicated a significant reduction in mean levels of absence occurrences, tardiness, part-absences, and no-calls. However, there were no significant changes in absence days and absence days per occurrence.

Leave Bank

The introduction in a medical center of the leave bank, a new time-off-with-pay system, resulted in a substantial decline in absenteeism, according to Kopelman, Schneller, and Silver (1981). Prior to the intervention the medical center offered its employees ten to twenty days vacation time depending on rank and tenure, seven holiday days, and twelve days of sick leave per year. Management became distressed when over a two-year period sick hours taken as a percentage of sick hours earned increased from 22 percent to 65 percent.

Under the leave bank, vacation days, paid holidays, and five days of sick leave were combined and called "paid leave." The remaining seven sick leave days were assigned to a sick leave account. As a result, employees still received 12 days sick leave per year. Similar to a "checking account," the paid leave account could be drawn on by employees almost at will. At the end of each year, a proportion of the paid leave account could be converted into cash. The sick leave account, intended primarily for long term illness, could be used only after the paid leave account was exhausted and with medical certification. In essence, it was similar to a savings account.

The new plan had the effect of rewarding employees with a longer vacation or cash payments for reducing casual absences. On the other hand, absences of more than five days cut into what was formerly vacation days and holidays. After introduction of the leave bank system, paid sick hours ranged between 12 and 22 percent of sick hours earned for a period of two and a half years, resulting in a considerable reduction over the previous 65 percent rate.

Well-Pay Plan

Under Harvey, Rogers, and Schultze's (1983) well-pay plan, employees in a nonprofit organization who incurred no absences for four weeks received a bonus of four hours' pay. Moreover, nonpayment of the first eight hours of absence discouraged casual absence. The plan provided protection against serious illness by paying in full any illness time beyond eight hours and up to two months, at which time a disability plan became effective. For the one-year period after the implementation of the program, total sick leave used decreased 45.5 percent and total sick leave paid decreased 55 percent over the previous year.

A negative aspect of the program, however, was an increase in average duration of sick leave from 9.6 to 20 hours. This can possibly be attributed to the program's encouraging employees to take more than one day off to minimize their loss of eight hours' pay. The amount of bonus paid under the program totaled $38,374. However, because of increased productivity and reduced sick leave usage, the plan resulted in a savings of $1,203.

Effectiveness of Mixed Consequence Systems

Based on existing, albeit sparse, research, the mixed consequence system appears to be a promising method for controlling absenteeism. All five studies reported positive results. Moreover, these programs generally have been found to have long-term effects, with post-intervention periods ranging from ten months to two and a half years, a considerably longer time than many of the positive reinforcement programs. Also, in two cases, savings were reported as a result of the program (Harvey et al., 1983; Kopelman and Schneller, 1981). Finally, improved employee attitudes were found (Harvey et al., 1983; Jordan, 1973; Kempen and Hall, 1977; Kopelman and Schneller, 1981). One study indicated that the reinforcement component of the program was responsible for attitude improvements; whereas the punishment component was critical in reducing absenteeism (Kempen and Hall, 1977).

It should be pointed out that several of the mixed consequence systems, including the leave bank and the well-pay plan, were designed to deal with problems of sick leave absence and unscheduled absence. The programs essentially eliminated the reward effect of sick pay—a factor that could be critical to their effectiveness.

IMPLEMENTING ABSENCE CONTROL PROGRAMS

Now that we have discussed a number of programs that have been used to control absenteeism by either rewarding attendance or punishing absenteeism, it is appropriate to deal with the issue of implementing absenteeism control programs. In doing so, we shall draw on the organizational behavior modification approach developed by Luthans and Kreitner (1974) (see Fig. 4.1). Based on the principles of operant conditioning discussed earlier in this chapter, this approach has five basic steps that allow diagnosis, problem-solving, and evaluation and is discussed below as it might be applied to attendance/absence behavior (Luthans and Martinko, 1976).

Figure 4.1
Organizational behavior modification problem solving model.

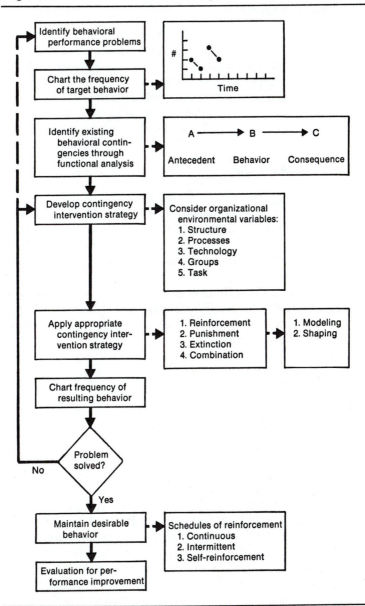

Identifying the Behavior

In this step the problem is identified. "Absence" and "attendance" are the behaviors of interest. As shown in Fig. 4.2, these behaviors can be broken down more specifically. For example, it is possible to identify contributing factors for absenteeism, such as tardiness, illness, transportation problems, drug or alcohol problems, or the beginning of hunting season. For the remaining steps to have meaning, it is important that the behaviors identified truly do influence absenteeism.

Charting the Behavior

In implementing absenteeism control programs, absence data are necessary to establish base-line data. These data tell us how often the behavior is occurring under present conditions. As the topic of measuring absenteeism was discussed thoroughly in Chapter 2, suffice it to say here that a variety of indices should be drawn on to determine the frequency of absence, how widespread absenteeism is, how concentrated it is, and the effect of absenteeism on production. Data should also be gathered on such organizationally-defined categories as excused and unexcused absences, absence due to illness and accidents, contractual absence, etc.

Functional Analysis

In functional analysis, the antecedent cues and consequences influencing past and present absence and attendance behaviors are identified. Antecedent cues are cues the employee associated with consequences of absence or attendance. For example, a memorandum announcing a contingent time-off program might serve as a cue for attendance behavior, and the opening day of hunting season (a temporal cue) might signal absence behavior. Other examples are provided in Fig. 4.2.

Consequences are identified by their effect upon the incidence of subsequent behavior. Reinforcers, both positive and negative, increase the frequency of attendance behavior. On the other hand, punishing consequences result in decreased attendance behavior. A similar argument can be made for absence behavior. Thus, as we have pointed out previously, what an organization has defined as a punisher, as in the case of suspending an employee for absenteeism, may in actuality *reward* absenteeism for some employees. Therefore, it is important to

Figure 4.2
Functional analysis of attendance and absenteeism behavior(s).

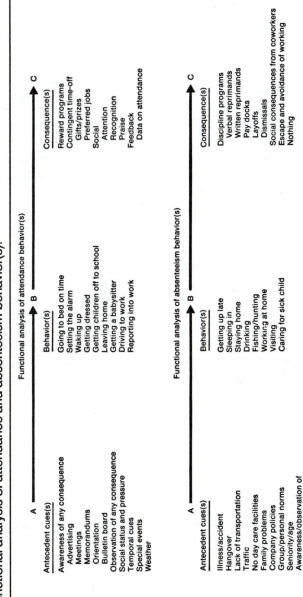

Functional analysis of attendance behavior(s)

A → B → C

Antecedent cue(s)
Awareness of any consequence
Advertising
Meetings
Memorandums
Orientation
Bulletin board
Observation of any consequence
Social status and pressure
Temporal cues
Special events
Weather

Behavior(s)
Going to bed on time
Setting the alarm
Waking up
Getting dressed
Getting children off to school
Leaving home
Getting a babysitter
Driving to work
Reporting into work

Consequence(s)
Reward programs
Contingent time-off
Gifts/prizes
Preferred jobs
Social
Attention
Recognition
Praise
Feedback
Data on attendance

Functional analysis of absenteeism behavior(s)

A → B → C

Antecedent cue(s)
Illness/accident
Hangover
Lack of transportation
Traffic
No day care facilities
Family problems
Company policies
Group/personal norms
Seniority/age
Awareness/observation of any consequence

Behavior(s)
Getting up late
Sleeping in
Staying home
Drinking
Fishing/hunting
Working at home
Visiting
Caring for sick child

Consequence(s)
Discipline programs
Verbal reprimands
Written reprimands
Pay docks
Layoffs
Dismissals
Social consequences from coworkers
Escape and avoidance of working
Nothing

Source: Fred Luthans and Mark Martinko, "An Organizational Behavior Modification Analysis of Absenteeism." *Human Resource Management*, Fall 1976, p. 15. Copyright © 1976 John Wiley & Sons, Inc. Reprinted with permission of John Wiley & Sons, Inc.

analyze consequences in terms of their *actual* effects as contrasted with their intended effects.

Some consequences that can be associated with attendance and absenteeism behaviors are shown in Fig. 4.2. It should be noted that this listing is by no means complete. For example, for some individuals, important reinforcing consequences for absence behavior are having a break from routine and gaining free time to engage in family activities and personal business (see Morgan and Herman, 1976; Youngblood, 1984).

In short, employee attendance is a complex behavior. A large number of reinforcers and punishers can be associated with either absence or attendance behavior. A complete analysis of the antecedents and consequences is necessary in order to design intervention strategies addressing absence problems.

Intervention Strategies

Developing intervention strategies to control absence behavior entails managing the environment so that attendance is followed by reinforcing consequences and absenteeism by punishment or extinction. The most effective consequences identified in the functional analysis should be considered for inclusion in the program. In addition, to the extent possible, steps should be taken to reduce or eliminate the effect of consequences that reward absence behavior or punish attendance behavior. Finally, other potentially effective consequences need to be identified.

The following questions need to be addressed if the consequences, whether positive reinforcement or punishment, are to be effective in reducing absenteeism:

- Are the consequences meaningful (that is, are rewards valued by employees, and are punishers intense enough that employees would avoid them)?

- Do the punishers and reinforcers offset any competing rewards for absenteeism?

- Are the criteria for achieving the rewards or receiving the punishment realistic and contingently applied to the majority of the employees?

In addition, special care needs to be taken to ensure that discipline methods are consistent with arbitral standards discussed earlier (Rosenthal, 1979).

One way of insuring that the rewards and punishments used are meaningful is to have employees participate in the design of the program. This can be accomplished by including employees or union representatives on the committee to develop the program. Moreover, employees could be surveyed as to their preferences for rewards for attendance. Further elaboration of procedures to identify valued rewards can be found in Luthans and Kreitner (1975).

In addition to manipulating consequences, it is important to develop strategies to deal with the antecedent cues. Antecedents such as family or drinking problems and illness are related to ability to attend, and strategies dealing with these antecedents will be discussed in detail in Chapter 6. The important antecedent cues to be discussed here are those that transmit information about the program. In this regard the organization should hold meetings to inform employees about the program, including the specific details regarding expected standards of behavior and the consequences for attendance and/or absence. In addition, clearly written policy statements should be developed and distributed directly to each employee, who in turn should be asked to sign a statement verifying receipt of the rules. Moreover, policy statements should be posted throughout the facility. Finally, feedback on the program, including its effect on absence rates, a report of rewards distributed for attendance, and disciplinary action taken for absence, should be provided regularly. By following these procedures, the organization will serve dual purposes of enhancing the effectiveness of the intervention and meeting arbitral standards for absentee discharge (Rosenthal, 1979; Scott and Taylor, 1983).

The appropriate administration of consequation schedules, as discussed earlier in this chapter, will insure that employee attendance remains at high levels. In traditional attendance programs, both continuous and intermittent schedules are in use. For example, an organization might require that employees phone in or have a doctor's excuse each time they are absent. At the same time, attendance rewards might be given intermittently, perhaps once every six months or once a year. The reward schedule used can differ, depending on the phase of the program. Initially, rewards might be provided daily. Then, as attendance improves, rewards can be granted intermittently based on further attendance improvement.

Evaluating Performance Improvement

Finally, monitoring the effectiveness of the program is a critical step. Measurement initiated in the second step should be continued throughout the program. Two questions are answered through the continuous monitoring: First, is the behavior changing in the desired direction? Second, is the intervention cost effective; that is, do the benefits achieved outweigh the costs? Results of the evaluation provide information necessary to determine whether the intervention should be discontinued and replaced with another strategy. Even if the program is discontinued, it is still important to continue monitoring behavior. Any program change should be treated as an intervention that might affect behavior.

In this chapter, we discussed absenteeism control programs that might be used to increase attendance motivation in organizations. In doing so, we introduced the reader to a theoretical framework, the principles of operant conditioning, which can be drawn upon in designing interventions. We also presented details of specific programs involving rewards, punishments, or both, for the purpose of providing practical examples. To conclude the chapter, we discussed implementation of absence control programs using an organizational behavior modification approach. In the next chapter, we present strategies designed to increase attendance motivation through creating an attendance-oriented culture.

Creating an Attendance-Oriented Culture

5

In addition to absence control policies, organizations have at their disposal a second set of strategies for improving attendance. These strategies have the same goal as the absence control policies discussed in the previous chapter (that is, to increase attendance motivation), but they rely far more heavily on voluntary behavior and the development of an attractive (as opposed to punishing) work environment.

Two general strategies can be utilized to develop a work environment that is more conducive to attendance motivation. First, efforts can be made to create a more inviting workplace where people *want* to come to work and participate. This can be accomplished through implementing realistic job previews and redesigning work to improve the fit between employees' needs and values and the reinforcers offered by the work environment (Lofquist and Dawis, 1969). Improved person–work environment fit, in turn, will result in more positive job attitudes and reduced job stress (Caplan et al., 1975). Second, attention can be given to changing norms so that they encourage more consistent attendance. Norms can be influenced by selecting employees whose personal values support high attendance, through clarifying expectations regarding attendance behavior, and by designing jobs where possible that are characterized by task interdependence. In this chapter, we will focus on three specific strategies: 1) recruiting and selecting employees, 2) clarifying job expectations, and 3) designing work. We will assess the value of each strategy in creating an attendance-oriented culture, thereby influencing attendance motivation. As discussed in Chapter 3, such a culture is referred to as a "moral" culture and is characterized by high salience and high trust (Nicholson and Johns, 1985).

RECRUITING AND SELECTING EMPLOYEES

Through establishing criteria for recruitment and selection, managers have an opportunity to shape the organization's culture (Schein, 1985). Therefore, if high levels of attendance are desired, then attendance proneness should be one of the criteria of recruitment and selection. What follows is a discussion of three approaches for using attendance proneness as a criterion in recruiting and selecting employees.

Recruitment Sources

A useful field study of research scientists and engineers examined the relationship between recruiting sources and absence (Breaugh, 1981b). The study found strong source-of-recruitment effects. Employees recruited through newspaper ads had absence rates twice that of employees initiating contacts on their own or recruited through college placement. Employees recruited through professional journal or convention advertisement had the lowest absence rate.

Differential effects of recruitment sources are thought to stem from differences in information provided by various sources. Newspapers and college placement have been suggested to provide less accurate and less complete information as compared to convention advertisement, professional journals, and self-initiated contact (Azevedo, 1974; Decker and Cornelius, 1979). As will be discussed more fully in the section on realistic job previews (see below), accuracy and completeness of information, in turn, affects job attitudes and behaviors (Wanous, 1975).

Results of this study suggest that organizations might benefit from examining the relationship between recruiting sources used and attendance and other desired employee behaviors. Based on the results of this examination, organizations can utilize those recruiting sources found to be most effective.

Realistic Job Previews

Conducting a realistic job preview (RJP) as part of the recruitment process ensures that job applicants have an accurate picture of the job and the organization (Wanous, 1975). The RJP presents a balanced picture of the job and the organization, including both positive and negative aspects. The purpose of the preview is to facilitate the matching process between the applicant's needs and the organization's climate (Wanous, 1980). Proponents claim that by providing applicants with an accurate description of the job, those accepting the job will be more satisfied and consequently less likely to leave voluntarily. Realistic job previews have been provided through oral presentations, through film or video, and through visits to the work site.

A recent quantitative meta-analysis of twenty-one RJP experiments reported that RJPs tended to lower initial job expectations and to increase self-selection, organizational commitment, job satisfaction, performance, and job survival (Premack & Wanous, 1985). The effect, however, was generally modest in size, with job survival and performance being the most strongly influenced by RJPs.

At least four psychological processes have been proposed to explain why RJPs impact job satisfaction and turnover (Breaugh, 1983). First, it has been suggested that RJPs result in lower initial job expectations, which are more likely to be congruent with what an employee actually encounters on the job. Second, RJPs might improve the employee's ability to cope with job demands, that is, "forewarned is forearmed." Third, RJPs communicate an "air of honesty" to applicants, who then experience greater freedom in choosing the organization. Because they make the decision without coercion, applicants are more committed to the decision. Finally, a self-selection process occurs such that if the job does not match the applicant's needs, the applicant will not accept it; those that accept are more likely to be satisfied and less likely to leave.

However, as stated by Breaugh (1983, p. 619), "Although it seems clear that RJPs can sometimes have beneficial effects (for example, reducing turnover), at present empirical data are lacking on why RJPs have the effects they do and in what contexts they are likely to be useful."

That RJPs are only modestly effective in decreasing turnover suggests that there are boundary conditions that limit their effectiveness. Breaugh (1983) postulates that RJPs will be more effective when the job applicant 1) can be selective in accepting a job offer, 2) has unrealistic job expectations, and/or 3) would have difficulty coping with job demands without an RJP.

Yet to be explored empirically is the relationship between providing RJPs and subsequent absence behavior. However, we concur with

Latham and Napier (1984) that providing RJPs might impact attendance, particularly if the content of the preview is expanded beyond giving the applicant a picture of the job to providing information about the organizational culture and policies. This information could include a discussion of expectations regarding attendance. If self-selection processes are operative, we would expect that cultural salience would increase. If the "air of honesty" explanation has validity, the RJP would result in a strengthening of the psychological contract. Hence, using RJPs might be effective in reinforcing a "moral" absence culture.

Wanous (1989) proposes guidelines that are based on relevant theory, research, and practical experience and can be followed in implementing RJPs. First, Wanous recommends taking a proactive posture toward RJPs. That is, organizations need not wait until there is a problem to correct. Second, an unstructured approach of diagnosing the organization can be used when time and cost are factors. Third, the content of the RJP should a) include as much judgmental material as possible, b) have an intensive focus (that is, focused on a few key factors), and c) include a medium level of negative information. Fourth, audio-visual methods of presentation are preferred over written methods. Fifth, for purposes of credibility, a job incumbent is preferable to an actor in presenting the preview. Sixth, introducing the RJP as early as possible in the selection process is desirable as only in this way can self-selection processes be influenced. Seventh, because of the extensiveness of RJP research, it is not necessary to implement a pilot study to initiate an RJP program. In suggesting these recommendations, Wanous cautions that research support exists only for one of the guidelines; that is, audio-visual RJPs are found to be more effective than written RJPs in improving job performance.

Past Absence History

One of the strongest predictors of future absence is prior absence (Breaugh, 1981a; Farrell and Stamm, 1988; Keller, 1983). In a recent study of research scientists, past absenteeism was found to be a better predictor of absenteeism than either work satisfaction, job involvement, or supervisory satisfaction (Breaugh, 1981a). Similarly, in a study examining eleven independent variables for their ability to add unique variance to the prediction of absenteeism, only prior absenteeism, group cohesiveness, and internal health locus of control were found to be significant (Keller, 1983). Other variables examined in this study were sex, age, tenure, marital status, number of children, job level, self-esteem, and job satisfaction. The measure of absence frequency has been found to be a stronger predictor of absenteeism than has the measure of total days absent (Breaugh, 1981a; Chadwick-Jones, Brown, Nicholson, and Sheppard, 1971).

In view of the fact that all studies have examined prior absence in the same organization, and not in other organizations, it is with some caution that we suggest that as part of the selection process, information be obtained on the past absence behavior of job applicants. Consistent with research on the validity of reference checks in predicting job performance, we recommend that the *previous immediate* supervisor of the job applicant be solicited as the reference giver (Mosel and Goheen, 1959). In view of Breaugh's finding that supervisor's rating of absence was highly correlated with absence frequency (mean $r = 0.85$), there is reason to believe that the supervisor's assessment would be a valid measure of past absence behavior. Finally, greater credence might be placed on references where the applicant's former job is similar in content to the job being applied for (Carroll and Nash, 1972).

Using past attendance behavior as a selection criterion has an advantage of being legally defensible. Such would not be the case if one were to use demographic correlates of absence, for example, age, sex, and race.

We would expect that the impact on attendance of screening out individuals with poor attendance records goes beyond simply eliminating problem employees. Such a practice would create a more salient absence culture in that new employees would hold values regarding attendance similar to those of present employees.

CLARIFYING JOB EXPECTATIONS

Clarification of job expectations in general and expectations regarding attendance in particular could also influence employee attendance motivation. As just discussed, expectation setting should occur during the recruitment process in the form of a realistic job preview. A vehicle for clarifying job expectations of new employees is the orientation program, either formal or informal. In addition, clarification of job expectations is associated with many of the ongoing activities of the supervisor, including communicating absence policies, measuring attendance, appraising and rewarding employee performance, and counseling employees. Thus, *the immediate supervisor plays an important role in creating an attendance-oriented culture.*

Orienting Employees

One important method of clarifying job expectations, once the employee has been hired, is through an orientation program. In a large-scale organization, the orientation program will be formal in nature. One component of the program should be a presentation of organizational policies, including attendance and sick leave policies. Written policy statements, perhaps in the form of an employee handbook, can be distributed to employees in conjunction with the orientation program. In a small-scale organization, the immediate supervisor of the new employee will take on the task of orientation.

Communicating Absence Policies

How absence control policies are communicated was found to influence unauthorized absence in one study (Majchrzak, 1987). Specifically, regular clarification and communication of policies led to a reduction in unit rates of unauthorized absence under certain circumstances. In particular, unauthorized absence rates were reduced only when the communication resulted in increased consistency in policy administration among managers and increased knowledge among unit members about the policies. Less important to the process in terms of affecting absence rates were perceived fairness, the severity of policies, and considerate attitudes on the part of managers.

Measuring Attendance

According to Schein (1985), what managers pay attention to, measure, and control is one of the primary mechanisms for shaping culture (see Chapter 2). Clearly, then, if a "moral" absence culture is desired, it is critical that immediate supervisors measure employee attendance. In fact, Latham and Napier (1984, p. 328) state, "From the standpoint of motivation, measurement in itself may be the most highly effective, underused, and deceptively straightforward approach available for increasing employee attendance."

The effectiveness of measuring attendance is exemplified by a study conducted at Parkdale Mills, Inc. (Miller, 1978). In this study, a daily attendance chart was posted where employees could see it. Each day the supervisor placed a blue dot next to the name of each employee on the job and a red dot next to the name of each absent employee. When an employee returned to work after an absence period, rather than reprimanding the employee, the supervisor welcomed him or her back. At the end of each week, the supervisor posted a weekly attendance graph, showing the percentage of employees attending work each day. Attendance rose from a fifteen-week baseline average of 86 percent to an average of 94.3 percent over a nine-week period. During the baseline period, reprimands were given to absent employees upon returning to work, and no comments were given to those with good attendance.

Appraising and Rewarding Employee Performance

If high attendance is a desired behavior, it follows that one of the criteria of performance should be attendance. In conducting the performance appraisal interview, attendance should be included as a subject of discussion. Moreover, attendance should be one of the factors in making pay and promotion decisions.

Counseling Employees

Counseling employees is a means of providing feedback to employees for good or poor performance (including attendance) on a timely basis for the purpose of maintaining or improving performance. However, having counseling skills is critical to the effectiveness of counseling, as employees might react defensively to negative feedback. In this regard, Latham and Napier (1984) suggest training supervisors in problem-solving skills useful in counseling. They propose behavioral modeling as an effective training methodology (Latham and Saari, 1979). Supporting this, one study found that employees supervised by managers trained in problem-solving skills using behavioral modeling had lower absences than employees of managers not trained using behavioral modeling (Wexley and Nemeroff, 1975). However, because preintervention absence levels were not measured, the causal effect of behavioral modeling on absence was not established.

In summary, through communication of policies and consistent policy application, expectations about appropriate behavior are clarified. The impact on attendance motivation would be greatest when communication of attendance policies is consistent throughout an organization's hierarchy and when the supervisor consistently applies policies across a variety of activities, as discussed above. As a result of consistent policy communication, cultural salience would be higher because the literal contract provisions are clear and known (Nicholson and Johns, 1985). Moreover, consistent application of policies would strengthen the psychological contract (Gibson, 1966).

DESIGNING WORK

Both job attitudes and work stress have been examined in correlational studies on absence behavior. First, recent meta-analytical reviews of the relationship between job satisfaction dimensions and absenteeism have uniformly found that the strongest relationship exists between work satisfaction and absence frequency (Farrell and Stamm, 1988; Hackett, 1988; Hackett and Guion, 1985; McShane, 1984; Scott and Taylor, 1985). Moreover, job involvement is more strongly related to absence frequency (average $r = -0.36$) than is either organizational commitment (average $r = -0.12$) or overall job satisfaction (average $r = -0.12$) (Hackett, 1988).

Second, studies examining work stress and absence have reported mixed results. Gupta and Beehr (1979) reported positive relationships between frequency of absence and role ambiguity, role overload, under-utilization of skills, and resource adequacy. Moreover, Galloway, Panckhurst, Boswell, Boswell, and Green (1984) found a positive relationship between overall stress from teaching and the number of one-day absences from work. On the other hand, Bhagat, McQuaid, Lindholm, and Segovis (1985) found that absence was not significantly related to either positive or negative job stress. And, finally, several studies have found absence and stress to be negatively related. In one study, job content stress (for example, participation, responsibility, quantitative workload, and threat by task difficulty) was related to reduced absence for technicians and blue-collar workers but not for top executives and registered nurses (Arsenault and Dolan, 1983). A second study found that although high role conflict and ambiguity were associated with greater emotional stress, high stress, in turn, was related to lower absence frequency (Jackson, 1983).

Several explanations can been suggested for the negative relationship between stress and absence. First, items such as participation and responsibility considered to be "job content stressors" in the Arsenault and Dolan study share similarities with the characteristics of an enriched job. Rather than serving as sources of stress, these factors instead might improve the fit between employee needs and job demands. On the other hand, absence and stress might be negatively related because individuals might feel unable to stay home from work when faced with high workloads and high levels of responsibility. Alternatively, absence might be used as a strategy for preventing stress from escalating, rather than as a recovery strategy (Staw and Oldham, 1978). Despite the conflicting nature of these findings, however, it is clear that the nature of the work itself, or work design, has an important influence on the attendance decision.

The design of work has received much attention in recent years (Griffin, 1982; Hackman and Oldham, 1980; Katzell, Bienstock, and Faerstein, 1977; U. S. Department of Health, Education, and Welfare, 1973). According to proponents of work redesign, the current interest has arisen from the disparity between the rising expectations of the employee and what organizations have been prepared to offer (Walton, 1972). A major factor contributing to increased expectations is the rising level of education. Over the twenty-year period from 1964 to 1984, the percentage of the work force having high school diplomas increased from 45.1 to 59.7 percent (Lawler, 1986).

Four general approaches to work design have been identified: 1) the mechanistic approach from classic industrial engineering; 2) the biological approach from work physiology and biomechanics; 3) the perceptual/motor approach from experimental psychology; and 4) the motivational approach from organizational psychology (Campion and Thayer, 1985). Our discussion will focus on two of these, the mechanistic and the motivational approaches, as these have received the most attention in terms of their effects on employee attitudes and behavior and organizational performance.

The Mechanistic Approach to Work Design

The current interest in work redesign is a response to the "dehumanizing" aspects of the mechanistic approach (see Table 5.1) of scientific management introduced by Frederick W. Taylor and other industrial

Table 5.1
The mechanistic job-design approach.

---

1. *Job specialization:* Is the job highly specialized in terms of purpose and/or activity?

2. *Specialization of tools and procedures:* Are the tools, procedures, materials, etc., used on this job highly specialized in terms of purpose?

3. *Task simplification:* Are the tasks simple and uncomplicated?

4. *Single activities:* Does the job require the incumbent to do only one task at a time? Does it *not* require the incumbent to do multiple activities at one time or in very close succession?

5. *Job simplification:* Does the job require relatively little skill and training time?

6. *Repetition:* Does the job require performing the same activity or activities repeatedly?

7. *Spare time:* Is there very little spare time between activities on this job?

8. *Automation:* Are many of the activities of this job automated or assisted by automation?

Source: M. A. Campion and P. W. Thayer (1987), "Job Design: Approaches, Outcomes and Trade-Offs." *Organizational Dynamics, 15*(3), p. 69. Copyright © 1987 American Management Association, New York. All rights reserved. Reprinted with permission.

engineers around the turn of the century (Taylor, 1911). The mechanistic approach has been the dominant approach for designing jobs in manufacturing organizations as well as service industries (for example, fast food restaurants, banks, insurance companies). The principles of scientific management include work simplification and task specialization. As a result, each worker participates in only a small part of the production process and performs repetitive, short-cycle tasks requiring little skill. Opportunities for social interaction are limited by the work pace, noise level, and the physical separation of workers. Many of the activities of the job are automated, and often the pace of the work is controlled by machines. Management plans how a task is to be performed, with employees having virtually no input into the process.

A number of outcomes have been attributed to this approach. From an organizational perspective, scientific management results in more efficient utilization of human resources (Campion and Thayer, 1985). With decreased training time, workers can be easily replaced. Moreover, because of work simplification, a high percentage of people are able to perform the job, and the likelihood of error is lower. From an individual employee perspective, the only "advantage" is a lower chance of mental overload and stress. Negative outcomes include lower job satisfaction, lower motivation, and higher absenteeism.

The Motivational Approach to Work Design

The motivational approach contrasts sharply with the mechanistic approach. The design principles underlying the motivational approach are shown in Table 5.2. Falling under the rubric of the motivational approach are job enrichment and job enlargement (Ford, 1969; Herzberg, 1966), the job characteristics model (Hackman and Oldham, 1980), and sociotechnical systems design (Cherns, 1976; Cummings and Molloy, 1977; Davis, 1977). As the job characteristics model and the sociotechnical systems approach are currently the most common approaches to work redesign, we discuss these in greater detail.

The job characteristics model

The job characteristics model (see Fig. 5.1) focuses on the relationship between the individual and his or her job. It is a comprehensive framework showing the interaction between task design, critical psychological states, and personal and work outcomes. At the heart of the theory are the critical psychological states, which are viewed as direct determinants of employee motivation and satisfaction. These are defined as follows:

1. *Experienced meaningfulness of work.* The degree to which the individual experiences the job as one that is generally meaningful, valuable, and worthwhile.

2. *Experienced responsibility for work outcomes.* The degree to which the individual feels personally accountable and responsible for results of the work he or she does.

Table 5.2
The motivational job-design approach.

---

1. *Autonomy:* Does the job allow freedom, independence, or discretion in work scheduling, sequence, methods, procedures, quality control, or other decisions?

2. *Intrinsic job feedback:* Do the work activities themselves provide direct, clear information about the effectiveness (in terms of quality and quantity) of job performance?

3. *Extrinsic job feedback:* Do other people in the organization (such as managers and coworkers) provide information about the effectiveness (in terms of quality and quantity) of job performance?

4. *Social interaction:* Does the job provide for positive social interaction (such as teamwork or coworker assistance)?

5. *Task/goal clarity:* Are the job duties, requirements, and goals clear and specific?

6. *Task variety:* Does the job have a variety of duties, tasks, and activities?

7. *Task identity:* Does the job require completion of a whole and identifiable piece of work? Does it give the incumbent a chance to do an entire piece of work from beginning to end?

8. *Ability/skill-level requirements:* Does the job require a high level of knowledge, skills, and abilities?

9. *Ability/skill variety:* Does the job require a variety of types of knowledge, skills, and abilities?

10. *Task significance:* Is the job significant and important compared with other jobs in the organization?

11. *Growth/learning:* Does the job allow opportunities for learning and growth in competence and proficiency?

12. *Promotion:* Are there opportunities for advancement to higher-level jobs?

13. *Achievement:* Does the job provide for feelings of achievement and task accomplishment?

14. *Participation:* Does the job allow participation in work-related decision making?

(continued)

Table 5.2 *(continued)*

15. *Communication:* Does the job provide access to communication channels and information flows?

16. *Pay adequacy:* Is the pay for this job adequate compared with the job requirements and pay for similar jobs?

17. *Recognition:* Does the job provide acknowledgement and recognition from others?

18. *Job security:* Do incumbents on this job have a high degree of job security?

Source: M. A. Campion and P. W. Thayer (1987), "Job Design: Approaches, Outcomes and Trade-Offs." *Organizational Dynamics, 15*(3), p. 70. Copyright © 1987 American Management Association, New York. All rights reserved. Reprinted with permission.

3. *Knowledge of results.* The degree to which the individual knows and understands, on a continuous basis, how effectively he or she is performing the job (Hackman and Oldham, 1976, pp. 256–257).

The psychological states result from the presence of the core job dimensions, defined below:

1. *Skill variety.* The degree to which a job requires a variety of different activities in carrying out the work, involving the use of a number of different skills and talents of the person.

2. *Task identity.* The degree to which the job requires completion of a "whole" and identifiable piece of work, that is, doing a job from beginning to end with a visible outcome.

3. *Task significance.* The degree to which the job has a substantial impact on the lives or work of other people, whether in the immediate organization or in the external environment.

4. *Autonomy.* The degree to which the job provides substantial freedom, independence, and discretion to the individual in scheduling the work and in determining the procedures to be used in carrying it out.

5. *Feedback.* The degree to which carrying out the work activities required by the job results in the individual obtaining direct and clear information about the effectiveness of his or her performance (Hackman and Oldham, 1976, pp. 257–258).

Figure 5.1
The job characteristics model.

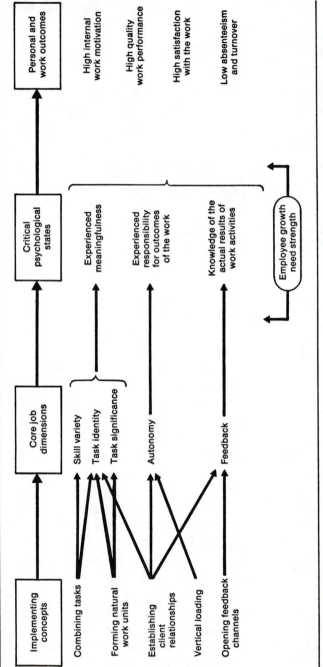

Source: J. R. Hackman, G. R. Oldham, R. Janson, and K. Purdy (Summer 1975), "A New Strategy for Job Enrichment." *California Management Review,* 17(4), p. 62. Copyright © 1975 by the Regents of the University of California. Reprinted with permission.

Skill variety, task identity, and task significance are seen as influencing the experienced meaningfulness of the work; autonomy influences the experienced responsibility for work outcomes; and feedback impacts on knowledge of the actual results of work activities.

The job characteristics model recognizes the role of individual differences. That is, not all persons respond positively to jobs high on the core job dimensions. Although the original model posited that people with high growth needs would react more positively to "enriched" jobs, the exact nature of the individual differences is still a matter of controversy.

As shown in the original model, low absenteeism was one of the personal and work outcomes resulting from jobs that are high on the core job dimensions. However, citing inconclusive research results, Hackman and Oldham (1980) in a later version of the model left out absenteeism as an outcome. Rather, they posited that competence of the employees whose jobs are changed might be a moderating variable. That is, increasing job scope might result in decreased absenteeism for more competent employees and increased absenteeism for less competent employees. An alternative view is that the relationship between job design and absenteeism is indirect through job satisfaction and organizational commitment (Griffin, 1982). In view of the research results on absence and job attitudes, another potential intervening variable is job involvement.

Two types of studies examining the relationship between the job characteristics approach and absence have appeared in the literature: 1) correlational field studies and 2) field experiments involving job redesign. Two meta-analytic literature reviews of correlational studies have examined the relationship between the core job dimensions and absence (Farrell and Stamm, 1988; Fried and Ferris, 1987). Combining measures of time lost and frequency of absence, Fried and Ferris found that autonomy, skill variety, and feedback exhibited relatively strong relationships with absence. On the other hand, Farrell and Stamm found identity to be a significant correlate of time lost absence, and task variety and significance to be significant correlates of absence frequency. Finally, motivating potential score, a summary index of the five core job characteristics, demonstrated a stronger relationship with absence than any of the individual job characteristics (Fried and Ferris, 1987).

In a narrative review of thirteen field experiments, Kopelman (1985) found modest support for the impact of job redesign on absence, with a median decrease in absence of 14.5 percent following implementation of job enrichment. Nine of the thirteen studies reported decreases in absence. It should be noted that Kopelman's review included job redesign experiments based on approaches (for example, Herzberg's job enrichment model) other than the job characteristics model.

In summary, based on correlational studies and field experiments, modest support exists for the relationship between task design and absence. Although the two meta-analyses report slightly discrepant results, the one variable that emerges as a consistent predictor of absence is skill variety.

Organizations that have implemented job enrichment include General Electric, American Telephone and Telegraph, Chase Manhattan Bank, Travelers Insurance Company, and Bankers Trust Company (Kopelman, 1985). Job redesign efforts based on the job characteristics model have been directed at both production and office employees.

The first step in implementing the job characteristics theory is to identify jobs to be redesigned. To do so, the Job Diagnostic Survey (JDS) can be administered to analyze existing jobs (Hackman and Oldham, 1975). Specifically, this instrument assesses jobs on the basis of each of the five job characteristics and the critical psychological states. Moreover, it assesses individuals in terms of growth need strength, internal work motivation, and job satisfaction.

Once jobs are targeted for redesign, five *implementing concepts* are drawn upon: 1) forming natural work units; 2) combining tasks; 3) establishing client relationships; 4) vertical loading; and 5) opening feedback channels. Each of these has an impact on one or more of the core job characteristics (see Fig. 5.1).

Forming natural work units entails arranging work into logical or inherently meaningful groups. In doing so, task identity and task significance are affected. Natural work units can be formed on the basis of geography, type of business, organizational department, alphabet, or customer groups. As an example, in one work redesign implementation that resulted in a 42 percent reduction in absence, the jobs of telephone installer and repairer were combined into one job, and each installer-repairer was given responsibility for a section of the district served by the telephone company (Segal and Weinberger, 1977). Prior to the work redesign, dispatchers assigned trouble calls to repair persons when they called in upon completing jobs.

Combining tasks increases both skill variety and task identity. Rather than performing small segments of the work, an individual performs all the tasks involved in completing a whole piece of the work. At Citibank prior to job redesign, the organization was structured according to functions, such that a single transaction would be routed among more than a half-dozen departments, leading to errors, lost items, and lack of control (Walters, 1982). Before redesigning jobs it was necessary to restructure the organization, a process referred to as "channelization," such that independent product organizations were established. The job redesign process resulted in each member of the clerical staff being given complete processing and customer service responsibility for a group of customers, whereas prior to the redesign each person completed only a small fraction of the job.

Establishing client relationships, such that the employee interacts directly with clients and has continuing responsibility for managing relationships with them, leads to increased skill variety, feedback, and autonomy. Client relationships often are created when natural work units are formed. Clients can be either customers outside the organization or other employees within the organization. Salespersons serving customers in a particular geographical region are an example of the former; an insurance clerk processing all new insurance policies for field agents in a certain geographical region is an example of the latter.

Vertical loading involves giving the employee responsibility and authority over work formerly reserved for higher levels of management. As a result, autonomy is increased. Giving employees responsibility for work scheduling, determining work methods, monitoring the quality of their work output, and finding solutions to problems are examples of vertical loading that have been used in redesigning work.

Opening feedback channels provides information to employees as to how well they are performing. Job-provided feedback generally is preferred over supervisor-provided feedback for several reasons (Hackman and Oldham, 1980). First, it is more immediate than feedback given by the supervisor. Second, it is more private, and interpersonal problems resulting from negative input from the supervisor can be avoided. Finally, increased feelings of control over the work results from job-provided feedback. Establishing client relationships, giving employees responsibility for quality control, and having employees maintain their own performance records are ways to open feedback channels.

Sociotechnical systems

A second motivational approach to work design is the sociotechnical systems theory. According to this approach, because of their interrelatedness, the social and technical systems must be considered jointly in redesigning work. Moreover, the interrelatedness between the organization as a whole and its environment is explicitly recognized. The goal of sociotechnical intervention is *joint optimization,* meaning that an organization will perform optimally only if its social and technical systems are designed to fit the demands of each other and the environment (Emery, 1978). Comprising the organization's social system are the people working in the organization, the relationships among them, and their expectations, attitudes, values, and needs. The technical system includes "the tools, techniques, procedures, skills, knowledge, and devices used by members of the social system to accomplish the tasks of the organization" (Pasmore, Francis, Haldeman, and Shani, 1982, p. 1184).

In contrast with the job characteristics model, which focuses on the relationship between the individual and the job, the fundamental building block of the sociotechnical systems approach is the *autonomous work group* (Herbst, 1962). For a work group to be autonomous it must contain within its boundaries all the functions necessary for accomplishment of its task. *Principles* underlying sociotechnical systems design include the following: 1) the design of the organization must fit its goals; 2) employees must be actively involved in the design process; 3) variances in production must be controlled as close to their source as possible; 4) work groups must be designed around relatively whole and recognizable tasks; 5) information systems should be designed to provide information in the first place where decision-making and action will be taken; 6) support systems should be congruent with the organizational structure; 7) human values should be considered in the design process; and 8) changes should continue to be made as environmental demands warrant (Cherns, 1976).

The sociotechnical systems design process involves a number of steps (for examples, see Cummings, 1976; Emery and Trist, 1978; Sherwood, 1988). One of the most critical steps is to develop a *state-*

Table 5.3
Example philosophy statement.

EXCERPTS FROM WHITE–MORSE PHILOSOPHY STATEMENT

The goal is to develop a society that encourages each individual to maximize his or her contribution to the objective of the organization while at the same time to satisfy his or her needs as an individual. Inherent in this goal is a commitment to accept that people are responsible and trustworthy, they are capable of making proper decisions related to their sphere of responsibility, and they can work together as members of teams with minimum supervision. They collaborate on such matters as operation maintenance, problem solving, and training and develop the power to act from within the group. In support of the goal is minimization of nonwork-related status differentials that usually develop in organizations today.

EXCERPT FROM CHEMCORP PHILOSOPHY STATEMENT

We recognized that special and patient attention would have to be given to establishing the management climate. If this were not done, the total effort would not meet our expectations. Without a favorable management climate, the competent people needed for the achievement of the objectives could not be recruited and retained. Furthermore, without a favorable management climate, the response of the people to the establishment of the objectives would be to neither accept them nor support them.

Some of the recognized important conditions in a productive management climate that would have to be cultivated are these:

1. *Mutual trust* between coworkers and among organizational groups at all levels.

2. *Freedom of the individual* to perform his duties his own way, so long as required results are obtained, and to express his own views without fear of ridicule or retribution.

3. *Openness* of everyone to questions and to suggestions about matters of mutual interest.

4. Acceptance of *accountability* for his own performance by each employee.

5. Mutual *support* for the achievement of shared goals among all employees.

(continued)

Table 5.3 *(continued)*

6. *Acceptance of change* and involvement in the change process at all levels.

7. Concern for the *welfare of the other person* in any joint activity.

8. *Restraint of harmful assertion of superiority ego* by the individual.

ment of philosophy regarding the desired culture and human values underlying the design process. This statement can be used to monitor whether the design outcomes are congruent with the philosophy. Human values that are mentioned frequently in the statement of philosophy include: 1) enabling employees to grow to their fullest potential; 2) establishing a climate of mutual trust; 3) minimizing status differentials; and 4) recognizing employees as being responsible (see Table 5.3). Value statements are widely distributed and displayed.

A classic example of a sociotechnical systems intervention is the case of the Gaines Pet Food plant in Topeka, Kansas (Walton, 1972). This new plant, which started operating in the early 1970s, was designed using the features described in Table 5.4. As a result of the intervention, fewer employees were needed to operate the plant than initially estimated (70 versus 110). Moreover, after eighteen months of operating, the fixed overhead rate for the new plant was 33 percent lower than in a comparison plant. In addition, there were 92 percent fewer quality rejects in the new plant, and the absenteeism rate was 9 percent below the industry norm.

The relationship between implementation of sociotechnical systems principles and absenteeism has been examined in one literature review of 134 North American sociotechnical systems experiments (Pasmore et al., 1982). Of 24 studies measuring absence, 81 percent reported reductions in absence. The most frequently used design features were autonomous work groups (53 percent of studies) and development of employees' technical skills (40 percent of studies). Decreases in absence occurred in 86 percent of the autonomous work group interventions and 100 percent of the skill development interven-

Table 5.4
Key features of Topeka work system design.

1. Autonomous work groups. Self-managed work teams are given collective responsibility for large segments of the production process. The total work force of approximately 70 employees is organized into six teams. A processing team and a packaging team operate during each shift. The processing team's jurisdiction includes unloading, storage of materials, drawing ingredients from storage, mixing, and then performing the series of steps that transform ingredients into a pet-food product. The packaging team's responsibilities include the finishing stages of product manufacturing — packaging operations, warehousing, and shipping.

A team is comprised of from 7 to 14 members (called "operators") and a team leader. Its size is large enough to include a natural set of highly interdependent tasks, yet small enough to allow effective face-to-face meetings for decision making and coordination. Assignments of individuals to sets of tasks are subject to team consensus. Although at any given time one operator has primary responsibility for a set of tasks within the team's jurisdiction, some tasks can be shared by several operators. Moreover, tasks can be redefined by the team in light of individual capabilities and interests. In contrast, individuals in the old plant were permanently assigned to specific jobs.

Other matters that fall within the scope of team deliberation, recommendation, or decision making include:

- Coping with manufacturing problems that occur within or between the team's areas of responsibilities.
- Temporarily redistributing tasks to cover for absent employees.
- Selecting team operators to serve on plant-wide committees or taskforces.
- Screening and selecting employees to replace departing operators.
- Counseling those who do not meet team standards (e.g., regarding absences or giving assistance to others).

(continued)

Table 5.4 (continued)

2. Integrated support functions. Staff units and job specialties are avoided. Activities typically performed by maintenance, quality control, custodial, industrial engineering, and personnel units are built into an operating team's responsibilities. For example, each team member maintains the equipment he operates (except for complicated electrical maintenance) and housekeeps the area in which he works. Each team has responsibility for performing quality tests and ensuring quality standards. In addition, team members perform what is normally a personnel function when they screen job applicants.

3. Challenging job assignments. While the designers understood that job assignments would undergo redefinition in light of experience and the varying interests and abilities on the work teams, the initial job assignments established an important design principle. Every set of tasks is designed to include functions requiring higher-order human abilities and responsibilities, such as planning, diagnosing mechanical or process problems, and liaison work.

The integrated support functions just discussed provide one important source of tasks to enrich jobs. In addition, the basic technology employed in the plant is designed to eliminate dull or routine jobs as much as possible. But some nonchallenging, yet basic, tasks still have to be compensated for. The forklift truck operation, for example, is not technically challenging. Therefore, the team member responsible for it is assigned other, more mentally demanding tasks (e.g., planning warehouse space utilization and shipping activities).

Housekeeping duties are also included in every assignment, despite the fact that they contribute nothing to enriching the work, in order to avoid having members of the plant community who do nothing but menial cleaning.

4. Job mobility and rewards for learning. Because all sets of tasks (jobs) are designed to be equally challenging (although each set comprises unique skill demands), it is possible to have a single job classification for all operators. Pay increases are geared to an employee mastering an increasing proportion of jobs first in the team and then in the total plant. In effect, team members are paid

(continued)

Table 5.4 (continued)

for learning more and more aspects of the total manufacturing system. Because there are no limits on the number of operators that can qualify for higher pay brackets, employees are also encouraged to teach each other. The old plant, in contrast, featured large numbers of differentiated jobs and numerous job classifications, with pay increases based on progress up the job hierarchy.

5. Facilitative leadership. Team leaders are chosen from foreman-level talent and are largely responsible for team development and group decision making. This contrasts with the old plant's use of supervisors to plan, direct, and control the work of subordinates. Management feels that in time the teams will be self-directed and so the formal team leader position might not be required.

6. "Managerial" decision information for operators. The design of the new plant provides operators with economic information and managerial decision rules. Thus production decisions ordinarily made by supervisors can now be made at the operator level.

7. Self-government for the plant community. The management group that developed the basic organization plan before the plant was manned refrained from specifying in advance any plant rules. Rather, it is committed to letting these rules evolve from collective experience.

8. Congruent physical and social context. The differential status symbols that characterize traditional work organizations are minimized in the new plant. There is an open parking lot, a single entrance for both the office and plant, and a common decor throughout the reception area, offices, locker rooms, and cafeteria.

The architecture facilitates the congregating of team members during working hours. For example, rather than following the plan that made the air conditioned control room in the process tower so small that employees could not congregate there, management decided to enlarge it so that process team operators could use it when not on duty elsewhere. The assumption here is that rooms which encourage ad hoc gatherings provide opportunities not only for enjoyable human exchanges but also for work coordination and learning about others' jobs.

(continued)

Table 5.4 *(continued)*

9. *Learning and evolution.* The most basic feature of the new plant system is management's commitment to continually assess both the plant's productivity and its relevance to employee concerns in light of experience.

Source: R. E. Walton (1972), "How to Counter Alienation in the Plant." *Harvard Business Review, 50*(4), pp. 74–76. Copyright © 1972 by the President and Fellows of Harvard College. All rights reserved. Reprinted with permission.

tions reporting absence data. In addition to decreases in absence, improvements in productivity, safety, quality, and attitudes as well as reductions in grievances and costs were reported in over 81 percent of the studies having data on these variables. Turnover appeared to be the least influenced, with only 65 percent of the studies reporting on turnover showing decreases.

The Relationship between Work Design and Absence

Decreases in absence were found for both the job characteristics approach and the sociotechnical systems approach. However, before drawing conclusions, we need to emphasize that the positive effects of job design on absence should be interpreted with caution for several reasons. First and foremost, experimenters have tended almost exclusively to report on successes rather than failures (Pasmore et al., 1982). Second, experimental designs used often result in problems of external and internal validity (Cummings, Molloy, and Glen, 1977).

The influence of job design on attendance can be understood by drawing on Nicholson and John's (1985) conceptualization of the absence culture. We would expect that implementation of the sociotechnical systems approach should result in a moral absence culture, characterized by high trust and high salience. The sociotechnical systems approach involves changing the culture, structure, and processes of the organization. The philosophical statement is in essence a reformulation of the psychological contract. Often, mutual trust is an important part of this statement. Operationally, trust is reinforced through involving workers in the change process, implementing autonomous work groups, and providing congruent support systems. The use of the autonomous work group and its associated high degree of task interdependence, in addition, creates a high salience culture. To the extent that achieving team objectives would be impeded by high levels of absence, we would expect attendance to be high in the organization implementing sociotechnical systems, and there would be little variation in absence behavior.

On the other hand, the job characteristics approach might or might not favorably impact the absence culture, depending on how it is implemented. Although increasing autonomy implies an increase in discretion, this might not always result in an increase in mutual trust. For example, if employees feel that their responsibilities have increased yet no pay increase has been received to match responsibilities, trust can actually decrease. Moreover, to the extent that redesigning jobs results in reduced task interdependence among workers, cultural salience can be decreased. Therefore, it is less possible to predict the nature of the absence culture when the job characteristics approach is implemented.

In summary, this chapter has discussed a number of management strategies for creating an absence culture consistent with high attendance. As discussed, some of the strategies are thought to be more effective than others; for example, we hypothesize that implementing sociotechnical systems design would affect attendance motivation to a greater extent than using the job characteristics approach to redesign jobs. Moreover, it is our view that for maximal impact on culture, the best results can be obtained not by picking and choosing a few of the methods, but by drawing on a number of the strategies and implementing them in a comprehensive manner. For example, using past absence behavior as a selection criterion; providing realistic job previews; and clarifying job expectations through orientation, supervisory counseling, and performance appraisal would be considerably more effective than using only one of these methods. Finally, our discussion was based on existing research and theory, but it is evident that often the research is sparse or inconclusive. Obviously, then, there is a need for rigorous evaluation of the effectiveness of the strategies proposed in this chapter.

Improving Ability
to Attend

6

Consider the dilemma faced by a single parent who is perfectly healthy and motivated to come to work but whose child wakes up in the morning too sick to attend school. What does he or she do? Oftentimes, the parent will stay home to take care of the sick child, thereby creating problems both for the employee and the organization.

This dilemma and many like it focus on the ability or perceived ability of an employee to attend work (see Table 6.1). When combined with the discussion in Chapters 4 and 5 on attendance motivation, a fairly comprehensive picture emerges concerning what organizations can do systematically to enhance attendance in the workplace.

Five major strategies to enhance ability to attend will be discussed. The first topic is *self-management training*, a recent approach to improving attendance by increasing perceived self-efficacy. Second, we describe interventions designed to improve attendance by *improving the physical and emotional health* of the employee. Included here are health management programs (such as stress management, physical fitness, and smoking cessation programs), restricting smoking in the workplace, and employee assistance programs. Third, *changing hours of work* are discussed from the standpoint of both reducing illness-related absence and reducing absence related to nonwork responsibilities. Fourth, *employer-sponsored child care* is discussed as an intervention designed to deal with absenteeism due to employees' nonwork responsibilities. Finally, *van pooling* is presented as an intervention to reduce absenteeism due to transportation problems. (Note

Table 6.1.
Programs that can improve ability to attend.

PROGRAM	AFFECTS:
Self-management training	Perceived self-efficacy
Health management programs	Illness
Stress management	
Physical fitness	
Smoking cessation	
Restricting smoking in the workplace	Illness
Employee assistance programs	Illness
Changing hours of work	
Shift work	Illness
Alternate work schedules	Nonwork responsibilities
Employer-assisted child care	Nonwork responsibilities

that what we present here are selected approaches to improving ability to attend rather than a comprehensive treatment of all possible approaches. For example, we have intentionally decided not to look at safety programs designed to decrease lost time due to accidents as these have been amply described elsewhere—see Grimaldi and Simonds, (1975).

SELF-MANAGEMENT TRAINING PROGRAMS

A relatively new approach that has promise for improving employee attendance is *self-management training*. Although this approach has been utilized extensively and found to be effective for quitting smoking, overcoming drug addiction, and improving study habits, it has just recently been introduced for improving attendance (Frayne and Latham, 1987; Latham and Frayne, 1989).

Self-management training is an application of Bandura's (1982) social learning theory, which recognizes the role of self-reactive influences in motivating an individual's behavior. According to the theory, a person can learn to exercise control over his or her behavior by arranging environmental contingencies, setting specific goals, and administering consequences for his or her own actions.

Training in self-management is hypothesized to be effective because it increases an individual's perceived self-efficacy and strengthens his or her outcome expectancies. Perceived self-efficacy is defined as the strength of a person's belief that he or she can successfully carry out the behaviors required (Bandura, 1982). High perceived self-efficacy, in turn, influences a person's actual behavior, including the amount of attention and effort focused on the demands of a situation and increased perseverance to overcome obstacles. Outcome expectancies refer to beliefs relating to the extent to which one's behavior will result in favorable or unfavorable outcomes. According to the theory, people with high perceived self-efficacy are more likely to act on their percepts when their outcome expectancies are high.

The implicit theory underlying the use of self-management training programs to improve attendance problems is that a significant proportion of attendance problems is the result of people feeling themselves to be ineffective in coping with environmental demands that prevent them from attending work. Moreover, they might feel that, even if they do change their behaviors, no change will take place in the low opinion of them held by coworkers or supervisors.

In a controlled study, self-management training was given to twenty unionized state government employees to increase work attendance. The training involved teaching participants to describe problem behaviors (for example, difficulties with coworkers) leading to absence, to identify the conditions causing and maintaining the behavior, and to develop specific coping strategies. Participants set distal goals related to increasing their attendance within a set period of time and proximal goals that focused on the particular behaviors necessary to achieve the distal goals. Trainees were taught to self-monitor their behaviors, including recording attendance, the reasons for missing work, and the steps followed subsequently to get to work. Finally, the trainees identified reinforcers and punishers that could be self-administered contingent upon goal achievement. Post-test results after twelve weeks indicated a significant difference in attendance between the training group and the control group (Frayne and Latham, 1987). Moreover, the difference in attendance between the two groups was maintained over a nine-month period (Latham and Frayne, 1989). Furthermore, self-efficacy increased significantly over the nine-month period. Finally, self-efficacy measured three months after the training was correlated significantly with attendance measured three, six, and nine months subsequent to the training.

Costs associated with the program included cost of the trainer's time and the costs related to trainees' being away from the job for the training. The training program consisted of eight one-hour sessions for each group of ten employees along with eight thirty-minute one-on-one sessions with the trainer. Therefore, the trainer's time involvement for twenty employees was ninety-six hours, and employees were in training twelve hours each.

IMPROVING PHYSICAL AND EMOTIONAL WELL-BEING

Absences due to illnesses and injuries account for nearly 60 percent of all lost hours from work (Klein, 1986). For instance, about 132 million lost workdays in the United States each year are attributed to the effects of cardiovascular disease (Maxey, Roy, and Kerr, 1982). In addition, being either overweight or underweight is associated with higher levels of sickness absence (Parkes, 1987; Zarling, Hartz, Larsen, and Rimm, 1977). Moreover, uncontrolled hypertensives miss work 33 percent more frequently than controlled hypertensives, and smokers are absent two to three more days a year than nonsmokers (Alderman and Davis, 1976; Bureau of National Affairs, 1983). Finally, it is estimated that 99 million workdays are lost due to alcoholism (Saltman, 1977). In view of these data, it is clear that strategies oriented toward improving employee health have the potential for impacting a major source of employee absence. In the discussion that follows we present three strategies aimed at improving the physical and emotional well-being of employees: 1) health management programs; 2) restricting smoking in the workplace; and 3) employee assistance programs.

Health Management Programs

Employee health management programs, a relatively new phenomenon, are comprehensive programs designed to effect a complete health lifestyle change. Components of a comprehensive health management program might include the following (Brennan, 1983; Higgins and Phillips, 1979):

- Comprehensive screening for the purpose of evaluating the employee's physical status, identifying health risks, and pointing out lifestyle habits that increase the risk of illness.

- Health counseling plan. Based on the comprehensive screening, the health counseling plan would set forth agreed upon health goals along with a timetable for achieving the goals.

- Exercise program.

- Stress management program.

- Smoking cessation program.

- High blood pressure control.

- Control of lipid levels, such as cholesterol and triglyceride.

- Weight control and fitness.

- Evaluation for the purpose of monitoring progress and modifying health goals.

A recent telephone survey of 1300 randomly selected organizations revealed that the majority sponsored at least one health promotion activity (Fielding, 1987). Moreover, about 88 percent of those worksites with over 750 employees offered one or more activities. Organizational interest in health management programs is due to such potential benefits as improved corporate image, reduced health care claims, decreased recruiting costs, improved performance, increased employee satisfaction and commitment, and decreased turnover (Driver and Ratliff, 1982; Terborg, 1986). In addition, absenteeism due to illness might be reduced as a result of these programs. With a few exceptions, however, evidence supporting these benefits is largely anecdotal (Terborg, 1986; Wolfe, Ulrich, and Parker, 1987).

Three particularly promising strategies for reducing illness-related absence are 1) stress management programs; 2) physical fitness programs; and 3) smoking cessation programs.

Stress management programs

The relationship between both work and nonwork stress and absenteeism has been supported in a number of correlational studies (Arsenault and Dolan, 1983; Galloway et al., 1984; Gupta and Beehr, 1979; Jamal, 1981). Absenteeism has been found to be positively associated with job context stressors but not job content stressors (Arsenault and Dolan, 1983; Gupta and Beehr, 1979; Tellenback, Brenner, and Lofgren, 1983). Moreover, absence frequency was reported to be negatively related to hassles (that is, experiences and conditions of daily living that are appraised as salient and harmful or threatening to a person's well-being) and positively related to daily uplifts (that is, those positive experiences and conditions of daily living) (Ivancevich, 1986).

In addition to changing characteristics of the job situation to reduce stress, organizations can implement stress management programs. Stress management programs can range from comprehensive approaches resembling health management programs to narrow training programs, such as biofeedback, muscle relaxation, meditation, and cognitive structuring/behavioral skills training.

A comprehensive stress management program implemented in a large financial institution included a twenty-minute health evaluation interview (Seamonds, 1982, 1983). The interview was designed to assess stress-related symptoms and coping abilities associated primarily with work stress. Those employees having stress-related symptoms were referred to appropriate programs and/or given educational materials. Referral sources included 1) career planning and educational offerings, 2) psychiatric consultation, 3) blood pressure and weight control programs, and 4) coaching and education programs related to exercise, biofeedback, and relaxation techniques. It was found that illness absenteeism dropped significantly as a result of the health evaluation interview and referral.

Recently, stress management training programs involving biofeedback, muscle relaxation methods, meditation, and cognitive restructuring/behavioral skills training have been conducted in the workplace and have been found to be useful in reducing worker arousal level and subjective responses to stress (see Murphy, 1984a and 1986, for reviews of the literature). Worker arousal levels in these studies were measured by forehead electromyograph, systolic and diastolic blood pressure, and hand temperature; subjective responses to stress examined included anxiety, reported ability to cope with stress, and psychological and somatic symptoms. The worksite support for the effectiveness of these methods adds to the already demonstrated clinical and laboratory support (as cited in Murphy, 1984a).

Two unpublished studies have examined the effects of stress management training on absence behavior. First, Riley, Fredericksen, and Winett (1984) reported decreases in absenteeism and increases in productivity for clerical workers during the one-year period following stress management training. However, similar changes were found for the control group. The second study found significant improvements in attendance ratings and reductions in total hours absent and Monday/Friday absences for a group receiving muscle relaxation training relative to groups exposed to either biofeedback training or no training (Murphy, 1984b and 1986). As this program provides a good example of stress management training, we will describe it in more detail. In this program, daily one-hour training sessions took place over a two-week period. During the first two days, workers were provided with stress education information on such topics as sources of stress at work, stress/health relationships, extent of control over stressors, and the potential value of biofeedback/relaxation training for gaining control over psychophysiological responses. Subjects received training in either biofeedback or muscle relaxation over a five-day period. During the last two days, participants practiced what they had learned during the training period. Physiological responses were recorded before and after each training session.

In making the decision whether to implement stress management programs, managers need to identify the sources of stress the program is attempting to ameliorate. Reducing the stressors directly would be preferred over a program designed to alter reactions of employees to the stressors. As Ganster, Mayes, Sime, and Tharp (1982, p. 541) point out, "Training employees to better tolerate poorly designed organizations would seem to be a less desirable strategy than one that attempts to make the organization inherently less stressful." However, some stressors might not be under the control of the organization, and, therefore, stress management programs can be particularly valuable as supplements to organizational change programs.

Physical fitness programs

About 50,000 U.S. companies have established some form of physical fitness program for their employees. Employer interest in physical fitness programs stems from their potential positive health effects. In particular, regular physical activity has been found to be associated with reduced risk of heart attack and deaths related to heart disease (Fielding, 1982). Moreover, employers who establish physical fitness programs do so with the expectation that illness, reimbursable insurance claims, turnover, and absenteeism will be reduced and that productivity and employee job attitudes will be improved. A final anticipated return to the organization from sponsoring fitness programs is an increase in the ability to attract competent employees (Falkenberg, 1987).

Measures of physical fitness as well as participation in physical fitness programs have been reported to be associated with reduced absenteeism in at least eleven separate studies (Bernacki and Baun, 1984; Baun, Bernacki, and Tsai, 1986; Donoghue, 1977; Fielding, 1982; Linking employee fitness programs..., 1987). At this point, however, it is premature to draw definitive conclusions regarding the relationship between physical fitness programs and absenteeism because of faulty research designs, including self-selection of subjects and non-equivalent control groups. Moreover, absence data generally have been gathered for the short run, leading reviewers to conclude that the reductions in absence found are probably more related to improved work attitudes than to improved health. On the average, studies have reported reductions in absenteeism compared with baseline or control groups ranging from about 0.5 to 2 days per year, with percentage decreases recorded as high as 50 percent.

Obviously, both participation in the program and "sticking with it" are necessary for physical fitness programs to be effective (Fielding, 1982). Participation rates generally range from 20 to 40 percent of eligible employees for on-site programs and from 10 to 20 percent of employees for off-site programs. Sticking with the program, once initiated, is a significant problem. Adherence rates are quite low, usually much lower than 50 percent during the first year. Also, those who need the program the most, that is, the high cardiovascular risk population, are least likely to participate; whereas those who do participate are generally over-represented by those who already exercise regularly and are in the low-risk category. Clearly, the program is more likely to result in positive outcomes if the sponsoring organization can devise strategies to attract high-risk employees to the program and to encourage participants to adhere to the program.

Employers interested in establishing physical fitness programs have a variety of options. These options range from educating employees about the benefits of regular physical exercise to establishing on-site fully staffed physical fitness facilities, an option pursued by only twenty to thirty (less than 0.1 percent) of the firms with physical fitness programs (Driver and Ratliff, 1982). An option lying between the two extremes is for the employer to cost-share with employees their initiation fees and monthly charges in private health clubs and physical fitness centers. Among the companies having physical fitness programs are IBM, Xerox, Weyerhauser, Control Data, and Metropolitan Life (Kondrasuk, 1980).

Smoking cessation programs

The leading cause of sickness absence is respiratory disease. In fact, one study showed that 40 percent of all absence episodes were attributed to upper and lower respiratory diseases (Ferguson, 1973). Respiratory diseases are more prevalent for smokers than for nonsmokers (Athanasou, 1975). In particular, Naus, Engler, Hetychova, and Vavreckova (1966) reported that respiratory disease was a cause of absence from work lasting longer than a shift for 40 percent of the smokers but for only 28 percent of the nonsmokers. Furthermore, chronic respiratory disease is more prevalent among smokers than nonsmokers in industries where employees are exposed to such occupational hazards as fiber dust, asbestos, and coal dust (Athanasou, 1975).

The 1979 Surgeon General's Report estimated that 81 million workdays lost per annum are attributed to higher rates of absence by smokers in comparison to nonsmokers (U.S. Public Health Service, 1979). Moreover, the report pointed out that smoking women had absenteeism rates 45 percent higher than nonsmoking women, and smoking men had rates 57 percent higher than nonsmoking men. For male employees smoking over two packs a day, the absenteeism rate was 84 percent higher than for nonsmoking men. Finally, the relationship between smoking and absenteeism has been supported in at least a dozen other studies (Athanasou, 1975; Athanasou, Reid, and Ferguson, 1981; Parkes, 1983).

The costs of smoking to U.S. employers have been estimated to be over $27 billion annually (No smoking: A profitable policy, 1982) or about $4600 per smoking employee (Weiss, 1981). Costs of smoking include 1) absenteeism, 2) medical care, 3) lost earnings to the employer due to sickness or early death, 4) accidents caused by inattention, eye irritation, and coughing, 5) higher fire insurance premiums, 6) lost productivity, and 7) damage to company property from burns, extra cleaning, and maintenance.

Smoking cessation programs, therefore, have the potential for eliminating one of the major causes of sickness absence and reducing other costs associated with smoking. Currently, the number of organizations sponsoring smoking cessation programs appears to be increasing. A 1981 survey of 313 employers ranging in size from small to large found that only 14 percent of the respondents had such programs (Walsh, 1984). A 1987 survey of 608 corporations employing large proportions of office workers revealed that nearly 30 percent offered smoking cessation programs. These programs vary in nature from distributing information to employees on how to quit smoking (referred to as "bibliotherapy") to physician stop-smoking programs and multicomponent group clinics. Multisession clinics typically were offered prior to and after working hours by such organizations as the American Cancer Society and the American Lung Association. Organizations could also opt to provide internal staff for the program. The costs for such programs range from $10 to $200 per person, depending on the nature of the program (Kent, Schram, and Censi, 1982).

Although the most common method of encouraging employees to quit smoking is to finance the cost of treatment, some employers have provided employees with other incentives with some success (No smoking: A profitable policy, 1982). These programs typically involve a monetary reward for quitting smoking, although the size of the reward and reinforcement schedule varies considerably. For example, a straight $7 weekly bonus to stop smoking was offered to employees in Speedcall Corporation. Over a two-year period, twenty-one of twenty-five smokers quit smoking. Another example of the use of incentives was the sponsorship of a competition to quit smoking among four banks located within one square mile of each other (Klesges and Glasgow, 1986). A number of prizes were offered, and the grand prize was a meal catered by the executives of the losing bank and provided to all employees of the winning bank. At 88 percent, participation rates were considerably higher than those usually reported in the literature. Moreover, 91 percent of the participants completed the program. Given the high participation rate, the sustained cessation rate of 16 percent was considered to be successful.

A recent literature review evaluated the relative effectiveness of four types of smoking cessation programs in terms of participation and cessation rates (Klesges, Cigrang, and Glascow, 1987). Incentive-based programs, particularly when offered in conjunction with a multicomponent group program, appeared to be associated with high participation and cessation rates. Although multicomponent programs resulted in high cessation rates, participation rates were generally low. On the other hand, physician stop-smoking programs had high participation rates but only modest cessation rates. Finally, least effective, but also least costly, were bibliotherapy programs, which suffered from both low participation and cessation rates.

Restricting Smoking in the Workplace

The second general strategy aimed at improving employee physical and emotional well-being involves restricting smoking in the workplace. Recent evidence indicates that nonsmokers exposed to "sidestream smoke" can suffer adverse health effects. Sidestream smoke, because it is emitted directly from the source, contains higher concentrations of hazardous and irritating substances than does the smoke inhaled by the smoker. Although as yet there is no evidence of higher absence rates, there is initial evidence of changes in psychomotor functions, increased heart rate, reduction in lung function, and higher incidence of lung cancer for nonsmokers chronically exposed to tobacco smokers (U.S. Public Health Service, 1979; White and Froeb, 1980; Hirayama, 1981; as cited in Kent et al., 1982).

With increasing evidence of the adverse effects of "sidestream smoke," at least four states and countless counties and cities are passing laws and ordinances that restrict the use of tobacco in the work environment (McKendrick, 1988). Typically, such laws and ordinances require the adoption of written smoking policies by employers. They can even specify the content of such policies. Moreover, even where smoking is not regulated by a law or an ordinance, employers who overlook the concerns of nonsmokers are confronted with a rising threat of litigation. The responsibility of employers to provide a hazard-free work environment has been legislated at the Federal level by the Occupational Safety and Health Act of 1970 and by every state except Louisiana. An employee whose health or ability to perform his or her job is significantly affected by tobacco smoke is considered to be "physically handicapped" under the Vocational Rehabilitation Act and applicable state laws prohibiting employment discrimination. Already, the premise that tobacco is both legally and medically defined as an occupational health hazard has been accepted in several court cases. In 1976, a California court ruled that cigarette smoke in the work environment was a contributing factor to a nonsmoker's disability, and the New Jersey Supreme Court forced an employer to provide a smoke-free work environment for an employee with allergies. More recently, in 1982, a Missouri court of appeals made a similar ruling in response to a petition for a smoke-free work station by an employee sensitive to smoke. In addition, workers' compensation or disability benefits have been awarded to employees who cannot perform their work in smoke-filled offices without injuring their health. Finally, employees who quit work because their health has been injured by tobacco smoke in the workplace or because they have a belief that smoke in the work environment affects their future health have been able to collect unemployment benefits.

In response to the proliferation of government legislation and the potential risk of litigation, employers have been establishing policies restricting or prohibiting smoking in the workplace. According to one survey, although only 16 percent of the 372 respondents had official policies regarding smoking in the office in 1980, 42 percent and 57 percent had policies by 1986 and 1987, respectively (McKendrick, 1988). Another survey of 608 large-scale organizations found that 68 percent had policies restricting smoking in the office in 1987 (Swart, 1988). As shown in Table 6.2, such policies vary considerably in the degrees of restriction on employee smoking, with the strictest being to hire nonsmokers only and to prohibit smoking both on and off the job. Prohibiting smoking in all areas with few exceptions (Policy D) was the most frequently adopted policy, being in effect at almost 40 percent of those with policies. The companies in the survey predicted that the trend toward adoption of policies that restrict smoking in the workplace will continue, such that by 1995 all firms will have a policy.

Employee Assistance Programs

The third approach to improving employee health focuses on offering employees needed assistance to help solve their physical and emotional ailments. According to recent surveys, about 18 percent of the work force experiences difficulties related to alcoholism, drug abuse, and poor mental health (Masi and Teems, 1983). Considerable media attention has been focused on the extent of alcohol and drug abuse in the workforce (English, 1983; Brecher, 1983). Specifically, it is estimated that between 5 and 10 percent of the workforce suffers from alcoholism, and between 3 and 7 percent uses some form of illicit drugs on a daily basis (Quayle, 1983). Alcohol and drug abusers can be found in all occupations. For example, of the 4.5 million employed problem

Table 6.2
Type of policy among companies with a smoking policy in 1987.

POLICY	PERCENTAGE OF COMPANIES
Policy A	1.2%
It is the policy of the company to hire nonsmokers only. Smoking is prohibited off the job, and smoking is prohibited on the job.	
Policy B	5.2
Smoking is prohibited in all areas on company premises.	
Policy C	9.7
Smoking is prohibited in all areas in company buildings.	
Policy D	39.2
Smoking is prohibited in all areas in company buildings, with few exceptions. Smoking is permitted in the smoking section of the cafeteria (or room with a similar function, if there is no cafeteria); in specially designated smoking rooms (smoking lounges); and in private offices, which may be designated "smoking permitted" or "no smoking" by the occupant.	
Policy E	26.3
Smoking is prohibited in all common areas except those designated "smoking permitted." Smoking is permitted in specially designated smoking rooms (smoking lounges). In open offices and in shared workspace areas where smokers and nonsmokers work together, where smokers' and nonsmokers' preferences are in conflict, employees and management will endeavor to find a satisfactory com-	

(continued)

Table 6.2 (continued)

promise. On failure to find a compromise, the preferences of the nonsmoker will prevail. Private offices can be designated "smoking permitted" or "no smoking" by the occupant.	
Policy F	18.4
It is the policy of the company to respect the preferences of both smokers and nonsmokers in company buildings. Where smokers' and nonsmokers' preferences are in conflict, employees and management will endeavor to find a satisfactory compromise. On failure to reach a compromise, the preferences of the nonsmoker will prevail.	

Source: J. C. Swart (1988), "Corporate Smoking Policies: Today and Tomorrow." *Personnel, 65*(8), p. 82. Copyright © 1988 American Management Association, New York. All rights reserved. Reprinted with permission.

"Smoking permitted" is synonymous with "designated smoking area." The latter term is increasing in usage.

A basic assumption is that all companies have policies prohibiting smoking in areas where there are safety and fire hazards and where sensitive equipment might be damaged. In reference to the scale above, the term "smoking policy" refers to a written statement or statements that place restrictions on smoking and intend to accommodate health concerns.

drinkers, it is estimated that 25 percent are white-collar workers, 30 percent are manual workers, and 45 percent are professionals or management (Saltman, 1977).

The cost of lost productivity due to alcohol abuse has been placed at almost $15 billion (Saltman, 1977). Although deteriorating work performance is a problem, the major impact on productivity of alcohol abuse is absenteeism (Trice and Roman, 1972). In fact, studies have shown that problem drinkers are likely to be absent from two to sixteen times more than the nonalcoholic employee (Quayle, 1983; Trice and Roman, 1972). Moreover, based on an average of 22 work days lost per year, it is estimated that 99 million work days are lost due to alcoholism (Saltman, 1977). In view of the fact that a General Motors study showed that alcoholic employees averaged 93 work days lost per year, this figure might be conservative. In addition to actual absence, problem drinkers display "partial absences," where the employee disappears from his or her work station during work hours, and "on the job absences," where the employee attends work in poor condition. High-status employees are more likely to engage in these behaviors than low-status employees (Trice and Roman, 1972). Finally, employers face insurance and benefit costs for alcoholic employees ranging from 3 to 5 times that of other employees (Quayle, 1983; Saltman, 1977).

There is some question as to whether alcoholic employees suffer higher rates of on-the-job accidents. Based on an extensive review, Trice and Roman (1972) concluded that the accident rate of the deviant drinker was no higher than that for other workers, except in the case of early stage deviant drinking. On the other hand, Quayle (1983) reported that employees with alcohol or drug problems have an accident rate that is four times greater than average, and alcohol abuse can be attributed to 40 percent of industrial fatalities and 57 percent of industrial injuries.

Based on a government-sponsored study, the cost of lost productivity due to drug use is estimated to be almost $17 billion (Brecher, 1983). Absenteeism, slowdowns, mistakes, and sick leave account for nearly 30 percent of the total cost, or $4.9 billion. Other costs of lost productivity are those attributed to drug-related deaths, imprisonment, and abusers leaving jobs for criminal careers to support their habits.

Industry has responded to problems associated with alcohol and drug abuse by establishing Employee Assistance Programs (EAPs) with current estimates of over 5000 programs in operation in the United States (Brumback, 1987). EAPs are designed to identify and provide treatment referral for employees whose job performance has deteriorated. Problem areas covered by EAPs include alcoholism and drug abuse, and emotional, mental, marital, and financial difficulties. According to a recent survey, alcoholism or alcohol abuse accounted for 37 percent of EAP problems; 28 percent involved family problems; 18 percent involved emotional problems; 8 percent involved drug abuse; and 5 percent involved financial/legal difficulties (EAP, Inc., 1984).

Employee Assistance Programs focus on problem identification, intervention, and recovery (Dickman and Emener, 1982). Key structural components of an EAP include written policies and procedures, an employee education program, a supervisory training program, and counseling and clinical services (Sonnenstuhl and O'Donnell, 1980). Responsibilities of the organization and its employees are clarified through written policies and procedures. Policies outline the company's program structure and encourage employees to take responsibility for their problems and to utilize available services. Also emphasized in the policies are prevention and early identification of problems. Strategies designed to meet these objectives are the employee education program and the supervisor training program. Employee education programs focus on teaching employees to detect the early signs of a problem and to seek help before a crisis situation is reached. In the case of employees failing to seek help, supervisory training programs teach managers to identify and refer employees for help using job performance and documentation. In-house staff can provide full counseling service or only diagnostic and referral service, the latter being more common as organizations move toward the broad brush approach.

In addition to the components mentioned above, a number of other factors are essential to the effectiveness of an EAP program. Among these are confidentiality and easy access, management and union support, insurance coverage, professional leadership, and follow-up and evaluation (Dickman and Emener, 1982).

Alcoholism treatment programs have been reported to be highly effective in reducing absenteeism, decreasing disability payments, and improving job performance (Alander and Campbell, 1975; Asma, Eggert, and Hilker, 1971; Dunne, 1977; Edwards, Bucky, Coben, Fichman, and Berry, 1977; Freedberg and Johnston, 1981; Norris, 1981). A 50-percent reduction in the number of absences was reported for officers participating in a New York Police Department alcoholism counseling program (Dunne, 1977). Five years after treatment in an alcoholism recovery program, 402 employees in a Midwestern telephone company had an absenteeism rate one-half that of five years before treatment (Asma et al., 1971). Moreover, remarkable improvements in job efficiency occurred with 58 percent of the employees rated as good five years after the treatment as compared to 22 percent before. Since 1972, 48,000 persons have been seen by counselors as part of General Motors' Substance Abuse Recovery Program. A 49 percent reduction in lost hours, a 29 percent decrease in disability payments, and a 56 percent decrease in sick leave costs were reported in a study of 117 hourly workers participating in the program (Norris, 1981). However, no improvement in absenteeism was found for a "high (medical and disability) cost" group after entering a health counseling program (Burton, Eggum, and Keller, 1981).

CHANGING HOURS OF WORK

In addition to self-management training and improving employee physical and emotional well-being, changing hours of work can also play a role in improving ability to attend. In this section, hours of work will be examined from two perspectives. First, the effect of shift work on sickness absence and absence due to nonwork responsibilities is discussed. Second, alternative work schedules are presented as a means of reducing absenteeism attributed to nonwork responsibilities.

Shift Work

Nearly 12 million workers (or approximately 16 percent of the U.S. work force) are engaged in shift work (Mellor, 1986). Most likely to work shifts are protective service workers (61 percent), followed by food (43 percent) and health services (36 percent) workers. Moreover, about 25 percent of operators, fabricators, and salesworkers are on shift work schedules. On the other hand, less than 10 percent of managers, professionals, and administrative support workers as well as farming, forestry, and shipping occupations are engaged in shift work. A recent study of shift work systems in the United States reported the existence of numerous shift schedules and many systems of rotation (Tasto and Colligan, 1977).

A shift work system is a system of fixed working hours with predetermined starting and finishing times. The most frequent schedule is 7 A.M. to 3 P.M., 3 P.M. to 11 P.M., and 11 P.M. to 7 A.M.; the second most frequent is 8 A.M. to 4 P.M., 4 P.M. to 12 P.M., and 12 P.M. to 8 A.M.

Among the alternatives of assigning workers to shifts are fixed, rotating, and oscillating shift systems. Under a *fixed shift system,* workers regularly work either a day, evening, or night schedule. About

4.6 million U.S. workers are assigned to an evening shift; 2 million work the night shift (Mellor, 1986). With a *rotating system,* employees are required to work the day, evening, and night shift in rotation. About 3.1 million U. S. workers are assigned to a rotating system. Rotation can be done on a weekly or other time basis. When the shift cycle is three days or less on one shift, the system is termed a rapid rotation system. Finally, under an oscillating shift system, workers alternate on a weekly basis between day and evening shifts or between evening and night shifts.

Studies have examined the relationship between shift work and absence from a number of perspectives. First, comparisons of absences have been made across shifts for workers assigned to fixed shifts. Second, in a similar vein, comparison of absences have been made across shifts for rotating shift workers. Third, absence rates have been examined for rotating versus fixed shift workers. Fourth, absence rates have been examined for workers switching to a rapidly rotating system from a traditional rotation system. Finally, variations in absence related to shift cycle position and day of the week have been examined.

Results of studies comparing absences across shifts for workers assigned to fixed shifts have been mixed. In most cases, studies have found no significant differences in absences across shifts (Colligan, Frockt, and Tasto, 1979; Fitzgibbons and Moch, 1980; Markham, Dansereau, and Alutto, 1982; Smith, Colligan, and Tasto, 1982; Walker and de la Mare, 1971; Watson, 1981). Where differences have been found, higher absences occur either on the night shift (Walker and de la Mare, 1971; Watson, 1981) or on the afternoon shift (Fitzgibbons and Moch, 1980; Smith, Colligan, and Tasto, 1982). Furthermore, in studies treating male and female employees separately, shift differences in absenteeism were found for males but not for females (Smith et al., 1982; Watson, 1981).

Studies comparing absences across shifts within a rotating or oscillating shift system have produced equivocal results. In studies of three-shift weekly rotation systems, absences were found to be greater on the morning shift by Shepherd and Walker (1956), Nicholson, Jackson, and Howes (1978), and Pocock, Sergean, and Taylor (1972) (one-day absences); however, absences were reported to be higher on the night shift by Pocock et al. (1972) and by Sergean and Brierly (1968). In a study of female food processing workers on weekly oscillating morning and afternoon shifts, Nicholson and Goodge (1976) found absences to be higher on the morning shift, a finding supported by Martin (1971) for uncertified but not total and certified absences. On the other hand, little differences in absences were found by Wyatt and Marriott (1953) for day and night oscillators. Finally, for workers on a three-shift rapidly rotating system, one-day absences and the inception of all absence spells occurred more frequently on the night shift and least frequently on the afternoon shift (Pocock et al., 1972).

Various explanations have been given for these conflicting findings. Both high day and high night absence have been attributed to the inertia that many workers might need to confront in order to show up for work at "unsocial" hours. In cases where day absence was highest, organizations had either a 6 A.M. or 7 A.M. starting time. In addition, high day absence has been explained by fatigue and lateness conversion (that is, financial disincentives or punishment for tardiness encourage converting lateness to absence). Finally, it was speculated that the high night absence found for workers under a rapidly rotating shift system was due to fatigue. The night shifts were always scheduled as the last days to be worked before days off.

Studies comparing absences between workers on rotating shifts and those on fixed shifts have produced mixed results. Workers on day shifts were found to have higher absences than rotators in four studies (Aanonsen, 1964; Taylor, 1967; Taylor, Pocock, and Sergean, 1972; Thiis-Evensen, 1958). On the other hand, other studies reported rotators as having higher absences than all fixed-shift workers combined (Jamal, 1981), day-shift workers (Brandt, 1969), and afternoon, day, and night shift workers treated separately (Smith, Colligan, and Tasto, 1982). However, Colligan, Frockt, and Tasto's (1979) study of hospital nurses found no significant differences in absences between rotators and day-, afternoon-, and night-shift employees, but rotators visited the clinic more than nurses on permanent shifts and took more days off for serious illness. The study of Smith et al. is revealing in that it is one of the few in-depth studies of shift work in the United States. In addition to sickness absence, other behavioral effects of shift work were examined. Workers on rotating shifts reported poorer sleep, altered eating habits, greater alcohol consumption, and greater incidence of work-related injuries relative to those of day workers. The authors attribute these results to circadian rhythm disturbances as well as social and psychological timing. Loss of attention, motivation, ability to concentrate, and a slowing of perceptual-motor processes all have been found to be associated with disturbances in circadian rhythms (Colquhoun, 1976).

A comparison of absences under traditional and rapidly rotating shift systems was undertaken by Pocock et al. (1972). A 36-percent increase in certified sickness absence and a 29-percent increase in uncertified sickness absence resulted after a change to a rapidly rotating system. There was no increase in absences for nonmedical reasons, leading the authors to conclude that workers accepted the new system.

A final temporal variable that has been examined in relation to absence is day of the week. Several studies have reported that the starting day of sickness is more likely to be Monday than any other day (Gordon, Emerson, and Pugh, 1959; Pocock, 1973). Moreover, uncertified absences were found to be higher on Saturdays and Sundays and lowest on pay day (Nicholson et al., 1978). Finally, higher absences were found on days immediately preceding or following days off from work (Markham et al., 1982; Nicholson et al., 1978). These studies point out how work schedules can conflict with other aspects of a person's life.

Based on the foregoing, it appears that shift work potentially has an impact on ability to attend from the standpoint of affecting absence due to illness and injury and interfering with nonwork roles. At this point, however, more research is needed to identify the conditions (that is, type of shift systems, hours of work) under which shift effects are likely to occur.

Alternative Work Schedules

Alternative schedules of work are increasingly being adopted by organizations with the expectation that job satisfaction and job performance will increase and absenteeism will be reduced. Two options, *flexitime* and the *compressed work week,* are the most prevalent forms of alternative work schedules. It is estimated that at least 2000 firms have instituted the four-day schedule for operating employees (Wheeler, 1972). Moreover, about 9.1 million full-time workers (approximately 12 percent of the workforce) are on a flexitime system (Mellor, 1986). About 12.6 percent of private sector workers and 11.3 percent of public sector workers are on flexible schedules. Moreover, men are more likely than women to have a flexible work schedule.

Although the compressed work week takes a number of different forms, perhaps the most common is the four-day and forty-hour work week with three days off. Another variation is the "eight-day week," where the employee works four ten-hour days and then has a four-day break (Newstrom and Pierce, 1979). A final variation is to compress both days and hours of work, for example, 3/36.

In theory, reductions in absenteeism should occur with the compressed work week because the extra day off provides time for attending to personal matters such as shopping or medical appointments. In actuality, research results are mixed. Two uncontrolled studies found reductions in absenteeism following introduction of compressed work weeks (Greene, 1974; Nord and Costigan, 1973). On the other hand, an increase in absenteeism was reported in another uncontrolled study (Steward and Larsen, 1971). Finally, two controlled studies found no significant improvements in unexcused hours of absenteeism (Ivancevich, 1974; Ivancevich and Lyon, 1977).

Several explanations can be offered as to why reductions in absenteeism might not follow the introduction of the compressed work week. First, it is possible that any effects on absence because of increased blocks of time off might be offset by the fact that being absent for one day on the 4/40 schedule represents a 25 percent increase over being absent a day under a 5/40 schedule. Second, a certain number of employees might use the extra time off to moonlight or take three-day vacations, which in turn might result in greater fatigue and susceptibility to illness.

There are reported to be more than 100 variations in flexitime, but all arrangements are similar in the underlying principle. Traditionally fixed times of beginning and ending work are replaced by allowing the worker a degree of choice regarding starting and stopping hours. Generally, though, all workers are required to be at work during a certain period of core hours. For example, under a county welfare agency's flexitime arrangement, employees were required to be at work between 9:30 A.M. and 3 P.M. They were allowed to begin work anytime between 6:30 A.M. and 9:30 A.M. and to leave between 3:00 P.M. and 6:00 P.M., so long as their work day totaled eight hours (Kim and Campagna, 1981).

Proponents of flexitime argue that allowing employees a choice in starting and quitting times will reduce tardiness and absences, particularly those lasting only one day. The discretionary time allows the individual the time to do things (for example, sleep in, go shopping), which under a traditional workday would have resulted in taking a day off. Other purported advantages include reduced turnover (rationale: conditions at work are better), reduced overtime (rationale: flexible hours enable a longer workday when the circumstances require it), and improved productivity (rationale: people will work during individually more productive hours) (Golembiewski and Proehl, 1978; Nollen, 1979).

Existing research supports the positive effects of flexitime programs on absenteeism. Petersen (1980) reported declines in absenteeism following the introduction of flexitime in eight of eleven organizations. Furthermore, Golembiewski and Proehl (1978), in a review of the literature, found reductions in absenteeism in eight of nine studies. However, only one study included statistical treatment of the data. Finally, four studies not included in these reviews, all employing control groups and three using statistical analyses of data, reported reductions in absenteeism on at least one measure of absence (Harvey and Luthans, 1979; Kim and Campagna, 1981; Krausz and Freibach, 1983; Narayanan and Nath, 1982).

In summary, for organizations considering the introduction of alternative work schedules as a way of reducing absenteeism, flexitime appears to be clearly superior to the compressed work week.

EMPLOYER-ASSISTED CHILD CARE

The proportion of the work force requiring child-care arrangements in order to work has increased substantially over the last twenty years and is expected to continue to increase into the 1990s. In recent years women with children under age six have been entering the labor force at a rate faster than any other group of women. In 1965 only 20 percent of women with children under six worked; in 1983 half of all mothers with children under six were in the labor force (Kamerman, 1983). In 1983 there were 8.9 million children under age six who had working mothers. Furthermore, a total of 13 million children under age fourteen lived in households where the only parent or both parents worked full time. The increase in labor force participation rates of all women, including mothers of young children, is expected to continue into the 1990s (Hofferth, 1979). Furthermore, the children of the baby boom era (1946–64) are now bearing children, resulting in a projected increase of 36 percent in the total number of children under age six over the period 1977–1990 (Rodriguez, 1983). By 1990 it is estimated that two-thirds of all children under age six will have mothers who work (La Fleur and Newsom, 1988).

Child-care responsibilities of working parents can affect work attendance in two circumstances. First, existing child-care arrangements can break down, resulting in a family member having to stay home from work. This might happen, for example, when school is canceled because of weather conditions or when the babysitter becomes sick or quits without notice. The breakdown of child-care arrangements is not uncommon: Half of the 1243 respondents in a recent survey had to make new child-care arrangements one or more times over a one-year period (Bruno, 1985). Finding acceptable alternative day-care arrangements can be difficult in general, but even more so for those who work during odd or fluctuating hours (that is, overtime, weekends, evening, or night shifts). Second, a child can become ill and consequently unable to participate in the normal child-care arrangement.

An indication of the effect of the breakdown of child-care arrangements on absenteeism can be gleaned from the Panel Study of Income Dynamics survey (Dickinson, 1975). Twenty-three percent of the families with children under twelve responding to the survey reported that someone was required to stay home due to a breakdown in child-care arrangements sometime during a one-year period. About 10 percent of those required to stay home missed work twice or more a month; whereas the preponderance (44 percent) rarely missed work (once or twice a year). The most reliable modes of child care were ones in which the spouse or a relative in the immediate family provided the care. The least reliable modes were children looking after themselves and sitters. Forty percent of families in which children looked after themselves and 32 percent of families using sitters missed some work due to a breakdown in child-care arrangements.

When a child is sick, particularly when child care takes place outside the child's home, a family member might need to stay home from work to care for the child. Children under three years of age have an average of 9.6 illnesses a year (R. LeRoux, 1982). On the average, the recovery period for a childhood illness is between four and six days. Staying home from work to care for sick children falls on the shoulders of working women to a very large extent. Fifteen percent of the women and only 2 percent of the men interviewed in the Panel Study of Income Dynamics reported that they were absent from work sometime during the year 1975 to care for sick children (Duncan and Coe, 1978). Women who missed work because of sick children were absent an average of 66 hours over the year; men absent from work for the same reason missed an average of 35 hours. On the other hand, a larger percentage of men (5.3 percent) than women (2.7 percent) missed work to care for sick spouses. Some of the men's absence might reflect child-care responsibilities usually handled by the sick spouse.

Options for Employer-Assisted Child Care

It is currently estimated that about 1800 employers currently offer some form of child-care assistance to their employees (Friedman, 1985). Among the options available to employers are: 1) child-care centers; 2) information and referral service; 3) child-care room; 4) after-school program; 5) summer program; 6) sick-child service; 7) reserving space in existing child-care centers; and 8) reducing employees' child-care costs. As we describe each of these options, particular attention will be paid as to its potential impact on absenteeism.

Child-care centers

In recent years the number of employers sponsoring child-care centers has been increasing. In 1978, 105 such programs were identified (Perry, 1978); in 1982, there were 211 programs (Burud, Collins, and Divine-Hawkins, 1983). In 1985, approximately 120 corporations and 400 hospitals sponsored child-care centers on or near the workplace (Friedman, 1985).

A variety of arrangements exists for these centers. Some are on-site, and others are off-site. In some instances, consortia of businesses, labor unions, and public agencies have formed to establish child-care centers. The administration of the center can be under the auspices of the employer, or it can be contracted out to profit-making corporations or nonprofit agencies specializing in child care.

Because traditional child-care centers often operate on a daytime-only schedule, sometimes charging penalties if parents pick up children late, employees who work odd and fluctuating hours confront special obstacles in finding child care. Therefore, a number of employer-sponsored child-care centers are designed to accommodate the particular work schedules of their employees (Trost, 1988). For example, America West Airlines' child-care center operates on a schedule of twenty-four-hours a day, seven-days a week. Also, nearly 20 percent of hospitals with child-care centers offer night or round-the-clock hours.

A child-care center that has received much attention is one sponsored by Intermedics of Freeport, Texas, a manufacturer of pacemakers (Friedman, 1980; M. LeRoux, 1982). The specific impetus for creating this center was high tardiness and absenteeism among employees. Opening in 1979, the Intermedics center serves 250 children or approximately 71 percent of the eligible employee population. Within two years of operation, turnover was reduced by 60 percent, and absenteeism decreased by 15,000 hours (M. LeRoux, 1982).

The child-care center is organized as a wholly-owned, profit-making subsidiary of Intermedics, but it operates at a loss, providing the company with a 100 percent tax reduction. After taking into consideration parent fees of $5 to $10 per week and the tax loss, the net cost per month per child is $86. However, according to Alice Duncan, director of the child-care center, the reduction in absenteeism and turnover more than pays for the cost of operating the center (M. LeRoux, 1982).

The North Side Child Development Center in Minneapolis is an example of a center established by a consortium of businesses. Spearheaded by Control Data Corporation, the consortium includes seven other companies, all of whom made an initial investment constituting local match money to obtain federal funding. When North Side opened in 1971, twenty infants and eighty preschoolers were enrolled. By 1977, expanding its program to provide after-school day care for children up to age thirteen, North Side served 128 children.

Of all the forms of employer-assisted child care, only the child-care center has been subjected to scrutiny with regard to its impact on employee work behavior. Evidence of the benefits of child-care centers comes in two forms: 1) testimonials (that is, claims not substantiated by systematic empirical research), and 2) empirical research (Miller, 1984).

The benefits to employers of employer-sponsored child-care centers have been examined in three separate surveys. The benefits, along with either percentages of employers reporting them or cumulative rankings, are shown in Table 6.3. Notice that in two of the surveys lower absenteeism was among the top three benefits mentioned. Moreover, increased ability to attract employees and improved employee morale were among the most frequently mentioned benefits.

In addition to Intermedics, discussed previously, Nylon Craft, Inc., of South Bend reported a reduction in its absence rate from 22 percent before the child-care center was established to "virtually zero" after the center was created (Hiatt, 1982, as cited in Miller, 1984). On the other hand, other testimony reveals that child-care centers have not been cost effective, and, in one instance, absenteeism actually in-

Table 6.3
Results of three national surveys of employers that provide child care services.

SURVEY QUESTION		
"What, if any, of the following changes are changes that have occurred as a result of having a day care center for employees?" Respondents were given a list of 7 items and were asked to indicate which had been affected by the child care service.*	"Which of the following items do you perceive as having been affected by the child care program?" Respondents were given a list of 16 items and were asked to rank the top 5 items that were *most significantly* affected by the child care service. Each item was then weighted according to the number and order of the rankings and a cumulative rank assigned. (Only positive items were listed, like "recruitment advantage," "less turnover," "lower absenteeism," etc.)[†]	"Would you say that the child care service has had an effect on any of the following aspects of company operation?" Respondents were given a list of 16 items and were asked to rate the effect of the child care program on each as positive, negative, unknown, or no effect.[‡]
SURVEY SAMPLE		
58 employers responded, most of which were hospitals with on-site child care centers.	204 companies responded.	Out of 415 surveys, approximately 178 businesses answered this question. The majority of respondents were employers that sponsor their own day care centers.

(continued)

Table 6.3 (continued)

Aspects affected	Percentage of employers responding affirmatively	Aspects affected	Cumulative rankings by respondents	Aspects affected	Percentage of employers responding affirmatively
Increased ability to attract employees	88%	Recruitment advantage	448	Employee morale	90%
Lower absenteeism	72	Improved employee morale	345	Recruitment	85
Improved employee attitude toward sponsoring organization	65	Lower absentee rates	214	Public relations	85
		Less turnover	211	Employee work satisfaction	83
Favorable publicity because of center	60	Attract persons on leave back to work	208	Publicity	80
Attract available talented employees	57	Attract available talented employees	205	Ability to attract new or returning workers	79
Improved employee attitude toward work	55	Improve employee work satisfaction	170	Employee commitment	73
		Better public relations	154	Turnover	65
				Employee motivation	63
Improved community relations	36	Better community image	137	Absenteeism	53

(continued)

Table 6.3 (continued)

Aspects affected	Percentage of employers responding affirmatively	Aspects affected	Cumulative rankings by respondents	Aspects affected	Percentage of employers responding affirmatively
		Less tardiness	88	Scheduling flexibility	50
		Improve employee motivation	67	Productivity	49
		Improve production efficiency	48	Quality of work force	42
		Availability of temporary help	26	Equal employment opportunity	40
		Tax advantage	14	Quality of products or service	37
		Provide equal opportunity employment	13	Tardiness	36
		Improved quality of product produced	11		

Source: Dana E. Friedman (1986). "Child Care for Employees' Kids." *Harvard Business Review, 64*(2), p. 30. Copyright © 1986 by the President and Fellows of Harvard College. Reprinted with Permission.

* Kathryn Senn Perry, *Employers and Child Care: Establishing Services Through the Workplace* (Washington, D.C.: Women's Bureau, U.S. Department of Labor, 1982).

† Renee Y. Magid, *Child Care Initiatives for Working Parents: Why Employers Get Involved* (New York: American Management Association, 1983).

‡ Sandra Burud, Pamela R. Aschbacher, and Jacquelyn McCroskey, *Employer-Supported Child Care: Investing in Human Resources* (Boston: Auburn House, 1984).

creased after a child-care center opened (Miller, 1984). Unfortunately, it is virtually impossible to draw any conclusions from these testimonials as the data consist of someone's "feel" for the benefits of the programs or numbers with no information as to how they were derived.

Three empirical studies of child care have been reported in the literature (Dolan, 1983; Krug, Palmour, and Bellassai, 1972, as cited in Miller, 1984; Milkovich and Gomez, 1976). Of these, only Milkovich and Gomez, comparing a group of child-care users with two groups of nonusers, found a relationship between children's enrollment in the child-care center and parent's work behavior. Specifically, they found that employee absenteeism and turnover rates, but not job performance, were associated with enrollment in the child-care center. However, because absence data were not collected on employees before their children were enrolled in the child-care center, we cannot be sure that the differences found in the groups were due to the child-care center or to initial individual differences in the groups compared.

In Dolan's study of hospital employees, factors associated with the content and context of the work were more important in explaining working mothers' absence behavior than utilization of the child-care center. Nonusers of the child-care center relied principally on relatives from the extended family group (mother, mother-in-law, sister, and so on) to care for their children while working. As was pointed out earlier, child care performed by relatives in the immediate family was the most reliable mode.

A final study, which evaluated a child-care center for government employees found that prior to opening the child-care center, employees who subsequently used the child-care facilities had higher rates of sick leave than those who did not. Moreover, although sick leave for both the user and nonuser groups increased after the center opened, the user group registered a greater increase in sick leave (Krug et al., 1972, as cited in Miller, 1984). Furthermore, annual leave for periods under eight hours decreased more for the nonuser group than for the user group. A major flaw in the study was the lack of matching of the two groups on some critical variables (age, marital status, pay, occupational level), which favored better attendance behavior for the nonuser group.

In summary, the evidence is mixed with regard to the effects of employer-sponsored child care on absenteeism. This is really not surprising. It would appear that employer-sponsored child care would have the greatest impact on absenteeism in the case where the working parents' pre-existing child-care arrangements were unreliable or of poor quality. On the other hand, employer-assisted child-care centers would have a greater impact on recruitment of new workers rather than absence of existing workers as it would ease the entry of parents with child-care responsibilities into the work force and enhance the image of the organization.

So long as the working parents' child-care arrangements are reliable before introduction of on-site child care, there is no reason to expect a reduction in absenteeism with employer-sponsored child care. In fact, employer-sponsored child care may actually result in greater employee absenteeism than other arrangements. This would be the case if children attending child-care centers have high frequencies of sickness due to greater exposure. Also, whereas most child-care centers would not accept sick children, thus requiring the parent to stay home, other child-care situations, such as family providers or close relatives, might be more amenable to caring for sick children. The employer-assisted child-care options that will be discussed next are more specifically targeted toward absenteeism problems due to a breakdown in child-care arrangements or sick children.

Information and referral service

Locating appropriate care for children of employees can be facilitated through an information and referral service. The role of the information and referral service would be to match a parent's needs for child care with an appropriate child-care provider. Services range from simply keeping an up-to-date list of family child-care homes and child-care centers in the community to screening the child-care options for employees.

Illinois Bell set up an information and referral service in 1970 for employees needing child care for their children (Friedman, 1980). Local neighborhood residents were recruited by the company to become family child-care providers when no suitable child-care arrangements were available. Illinois Bell staff members helped the family child-care recruits to obtain a license and provided training staffed by the Erickson Institute. In a two-year period, 473 Illinois Bell employees were assisted with their child-care problems.

An information and referral program can provide the employer with valuable information regarding employee preferences for child care and the availability of child-care services in the community. This information can be used to plan for future involvement in employer-assisted child care, such as establishing an on-site child-care facility.

Information and referral services appear to be particularly useful in reducing absenteeism caused by a breakdown in existing child-care arrangements. First, the service will reduce any delay in identifying another appropriate arrangement. Second, the organization has the information to anticipate a shortage of child-care providers and thus can take steps to ensure an adequate supply.

Child-care room

An approach that could be taken by small businesses would be to set up a child-care room stocked with toys and games. School-age children could accompany parents to work on days when school was closed due to bad weather, teacher conferences, and winter vacation.

After-school programs

In some cases, it is often more difficult for parents to find arrangements for after-school care for older children than to find full-day programs for younger children. Employers have two options: 1) establish their own after-school program, or 2) contract with others to do so. Often, after-school programs can be located in local public schools.

Summer program

When school is closed during the summer months, parents can be particularly wary of having children of all ages at home for long periods of time unsupervised. Providing a daily summer program, as was done by Fel-Pro Industries of Skokie, Illinois, is one possible solution to this problem (Friedman, 1980). In 1973, Fel-Pro began operating a nine-week summer camp program for school-age children of employees. Approximately 240 children accompanied their parents to work in the morning. From there, a company bus transported the children to the camp site, located on 220 acres of Fel-Pro-owned forest preserve property forty miles from the work site. Cost to the parent for the program, subsidized by Fel-Pro, was $10 per week. An alternative to a company-operated program would be to contract with a local community agency, such as the YWCA, to provide the program. Older children of employees could be hired as counselors for these programs.

Sick child care

What to do when a child is sick is a major dilemma for working parents. Under state and federal guidelines, sick children cannot attend a certified child-care center. Moreover, family child-care providers are often reluctant to care for sick children during the contagious stage for fear of exposing other children. Finding an emergency babysitter is extremely difficult, and hiring a nurse is financially prohibitive for most parents. Hence, either the sick child stays home alone or one of the parents has to stay home with the child. An employer-sponsored sick child-care program could, if not eliminate employee absenteeism due to sick children, at least reduce the amount of time taken off by parents per illness episode.

Several options are available for establishing such a program. First, an employer could support or establish a child-care center for sick children, as exemplified by Wheezles and Sneezles Day Care Center in Albany, California (R. LeRoux, 1982). Children of University of California employees and students who have upper respiratory and other mild illnesses are given special care. They are kept in a subdued environment and administered medicines according to parents' instructions. Children admitted to the center are screened by a registered nurse to ensure that their illnesses are beyond the contagious stage.

A second option is an employer-sponsored in-home care program for sick children. A local agency could be contracted by the employer to send health care workers into the home. This has several advantages over group care solutions: It is more convenient for the parent, more comfortable for the child, and more protective of other children. Providing such a service since 1975 to Minneapolis, Minnesota, employers and residents is Child Care Services, Inc. The service, operated much like a temporary help agency, has a twenty-four-hour answering service and five health care workers on call for work between 6:30 A.M. and 10:30 P.M. Although their $65 a day fee is prohibitively expensive for most individuals, for employers it represents a savings in contrast to having the employee miss a day's work.

Reserving spaces in existing centers

In a tight child-care supply market, reserving spaces in existing child-care centers can be a viable strategy for an employer with only a handful of employees needing services. In this way, the employer is assured that space will be available for employees should a breakdown occur in their existing child-care arrangements. The employer pays for the slots and then charges the employee whatever it chooses.

Reducing employees' child-care costs

Approximately 900 corporations currently provide some form of financial assistance for employees' child-care needs (Friedman, 1985). On the face of it, reducing an employee's child-care costs would not seem to benefit the organization so much as the employee. That is, employer assistance with child-care costs enables parents to place their children in quality child-care situations. However, the organization might benefit indirectly. It might be conjectured that because parents would not be worrying or suffering guilt over less than satisfactory child-care arrangements, productivity and attendance would be higher.

In a number of the programs where employers directly deliver child-care services, such as on-site child care and summer programs, employer subsidy is a component of the program. In addition, when direct service is not provided by the employer, employers have a number of alternatives for reducing employees' child-care costs, including 1) discount programs; 2) discount plus subsidy programs; 3) voucher programs; 4) cafeteria-style flexible benefits programs; and 5) flexible spending account programs (Friedman, 1985).

The discount program is an option pursued by an estimated 150 employers. Under this option, the employer negotiates with the child-care provider a reduced tuition rate for employees. Although there is no cost to the employer in this instance, the employee can save as much as $300 per year depending on the discount.

Under a second option, the vendor approach, the employer negotiates a reduced rate from the child-care provider along with offering a subsidy, usually about 10 percent of child-care costs, to employees. About 150 employers provide this option to their employees.

A third option, the voucher approach, gives the employee greater choice in selecting a child-care arrangement than either of the first two options. Here, the employer provides vouchers worth a certain dollar value to employees to pay for the child-care arrangement selected by the employee. Organizations offering vouchers frequently do so on a sliding scale based on family income. Among the twenty-five corporations currently offering financial assistance through the voucher approach are Polaroid, Baxter Travenol, and the Ford Foundation (Friedman, 1985).

Providing child-care subsidies can create a concern over equity of benefits. To offset this possibility, companies might consider instituting a flexible benefits program, called the "cafeteria plan." Under a flexible benefits program, each employee receives a fixed core of benefits and then chooses additional benefits from among a number of alternatives. Child-care services can be one of the possible alternatives. It is estimated that 75 major corporations and 500 medium-sized companies offer dependent care as an option in their flexible benefits programs (Friedman, 1985).

Finally, the flexible spending account is a reserve of funds available to employees to cover the costs of benefit options that are not included in the regular benefits package. Along with employer contributions, most plans incorporate salary reduction as a means of funding the flexible spending account. The flexible spending account is generally less complex and has lower administrative costs as compared to the cafeteria style program. Nearly 1000 employers, including between 300 and 500 corporations, have established flexible spending accounts.

In summary, a variety of options are available for employers wanting to provide child-care assistance to their employees. These options range from full employer involvement in establishing an on-site child-care program to minimal involvement by merely subsidizing child-care expenses. These options can have varying effects on employee absenteeism depending on the needs of employees. In the next section, we discuss how an employer can determine whether child-care assistance is appropriate for its organization.

Assessing Child-Care Needs

In deciding whether to implement employer-assisted child care for the purpose of reducing absenteeism, it is necessary to perform a needs assessment. In addition to gathering information on child-care services available in the community, the employer should survey employees to ascertain the suitability of existing child-care arrangements. In particular, questions should be asked to determine whether child-care problems caused employees to be absent from work. Examples of questions that might be asked are shown in Table 6.4 (see also Friedman, 1987). On the basis of the data gathered in the needs assessment, the employer can estimate how much of an impact implementation of employer-assisted child care will have on absenteeism. If it is determined that employer-assisted child care will have a favorable impact, then programs compatible with employee preferences can be designed and implemented.

Table 6.4
Need assessment questions.

A. Have you missed work during the past six months because:

_____	child was ill?	Number of days: _____
_____	sitter was ill?	Number of days: _____
_____	needed to find new child care arrangements?	Number of days: _____
_____	other child care problems?	_____

B. Were you late for work during the past six months because of child care problems?

_____ No

_____ Yes   How many times?   _____

                    Describe the problem(s):   _____

                    _____

C. Have you left work early during the past six months because of child care problems?

_____ No

_____ Yes   How many times? _____

                    Describe the problem(s):   _____

                    _____

Source: Perry, K. S. (1982), *Employers and Child Care: Establishing Services Through the Workplace.* (Pamphlet #23). Washington, D.C.: U.S.D.O.L. Women's Bureau.

VAN POOLING

The final mechanism available to many employees to enhance ability to attend is van pooling. Transportation problems can be an important cause of absenteeism, particularly when either long distances or long commuting times are required. Poor weather conditions and lack of automobile ownership can also be factors contributing to transportation problems. Finally, as noted in Chapter 4, the problem can be exacerbated further by organizational policies for disciplining tardiness.

Encouraging and helping employees to share rides in vans is an innovative approach taken by more than 1000 employers to deal with transportation problems (Ride sharing..., 1984). An estimated 276,000 people van pool to work every day in some 23,000 vans (Van pooling progress continues, 1983). And the numbers of people involved in van pooling continue to grow. Since 1981 there has been an estimated 40 percent increase in van pooling. Van pool operations vary in size from single van operations to the 464-van fleet operated by Prudential Insurance Company. Companies either operate van pools on their own or lease the vans from a third party, such as Metropool, located in Stamford, Connecticut.

The basic concept of van pooling is similar to that of car pooling. Employees living close to each other are picked up each morning by another employee who drives the van. The administrative costs of the van pool program are generally borne by the company, but the van riders pay the van's operating expenses. The driver generally either rides free and/or can use the van for personal activities during off-duty hours.

It would be misleading to suggest that organizations are encouraging van pooling principally to reduce absenteeism. In fact, other potentially more important benefits can accrue to the organization. A planned expansion of parking facilities might no longer be necessary— 3M Company saved $3.5 million in this way (Ride sharing . . ., 1984). Traffic congestion can be reduced around offices and factories. And, of course, employee punctuality and morale can be improved. All this is in addition to the benefits to society of gasoline savings and elimination of pollutants in the air.

Even though employees pay the operating costs of van pooling, they view van pooling as a fringe benefit. Employee commuting costs, including parking-lot fees and gasoline expenses, are cut considerably. Moreover, the nondriving employee has a more relaxing commute.

In this chapter, programs that can improve ability to attend work were discussed. Among these were self-management training programs, employee health management programs, restricting smoking in the work place, employee assistance programs, changing hours of work, employer-assisted day care, and van pooling. Although these programs would appear to impact some of the causal factors placing constraints on ability to attend work, for the most part there is a lack of rigorous research demonstrating their effects on reducing absence. Also, we should caution that these programs might not be appropriate for all organizations; their appropriateness depends on the particular constraints on attendance faced by the employees. Finally, we have attempted to point out that in addition to improved attendance, there can be other benefits to these programs. Therefore, organizational implementation of such programs should only follow a careful diagnosis of the causes of absence and an assessment of all costs and benefits associated with the implementation. Moreover, critical to implementation is careful evaluation of the program.

Managing Employee Absenteeism: A Summary

7

We now come to the end of our analysis of employee absenteeism. We have tried throughout this assessment to develop a better understanding of what we know — and what we do not know — about absence processes in organizations. If there is a lesson to be learned from our analysis it is that managers and organizations can do something to reduce absence at work if they are willing to approach the problem systematically and constructively. This conclusion should be evident from a review of the foregoing chapters.

At the beginning of the book, we examined several propositions about absence behavior. It was noted that absenteeism is both expensive and pervasive. It is indeed an international problem, although the extent varies from country to country. Numerous "determinants" of absenteeism can be identified, and several positive and negative consequences typically follow as a result of absences. It was also noted in Chapter 1 that there are problems with both the meaning and the measurement of absenteeism. That is, absence means different things to different people, and there are various — and not always related — ways to measure the behavior.

In Chapter 2, we explored assessment techniques in some detail. Included here were both the reasons for collecting absence data and different methods for accomplishing this task. In addition, methods of determining overall costs of absenteeism to the organization were discussed.

Throughout the history of research on this subject, several attempts have been made to bring together the disparate research findings into a reasonably cogent and coherent model. Such models can assist both in guiding future research and in serving as an aid to managers hoping to solve the problem. The developmental sequence of these models was discussed in Chapter 3. Several early attempts at model building were reviewed, followed by a more detailed review of two integrative models. Recent research was examined as it relates to these models, and lessons for future modeling efforts were summarized.

Following this, a new diagnostic model of employee absenteeism was introduced (see Fig. 3.5). This new model attempts to draw upon the more recent research in the field and incorporates both avoidable and unavoidable influences on absence. In general, the model is divided into two parts: factors like organizational practices and absence culture that influence attendance motivation, and factors like perceived ability to attend that combine with attendance motivation ultimately to determine actual attendance. The model further specifies a series of feedback loops and highlights the importance of variations in societal context (for example, differences in social norms both across and within cultures, changes in labor markets or economic conditions) in such processes. Throughout the model, emphasis is placed on the interactive dynamics between individual characteristics, group forces such as absence culture, and organizational/managerial practices as they jointly determine an employee's desire and ability to attend. It is hoped that the new model will serve as a stimulus to researchers to continue their explorations on this important topic, as well as an aid to managers interested in better managing the absence process in their own organizations.

To help in this process, the next three chapters (Chapters 4, 5, and 6) examined what we know about how to reduce absence on the job. The focus here was on strategies for problem resolution. Thus, on the basis of the conceptual models presented in Chapter 3, we moved in Chapter 4 to a detailed assessment of the use of absence control policies in organizations. Positive reinforcement, negative reinforcement, and punishment programs were reviewed, and the effectiveness of each was discussed. For instance, attendance can oftentimes be improved when companies offer incentives for good attendance. Moreover, attendance can also be improved at times through the use of progressive discipline for the more recalcitrant employees. Specific mechanisms for implementing absence control systems were also discussed in this chapter.

This was followed in Chapter 5 by a review of the methods by which managers can create an attendance-oriented work culture, instead of an absence-oriented one. It was noted, for example, that managers can incorporate an absence consciousness in their approach to recruitment and selection, in the standards and expectations they set for employees, and in work redesign efforts. By clearly establishing attendance-oriented norms and expectations, and then reinforcing these expectations with a constructive, meaningful work environment, many companies have discovered that much of the problem disappears.

Finally, in Chapter 6 we discussed methods that pertain to enhancing employees' ability to attend. The focus here was on techniques that can be implemented that make it easier for people to overcome potential obstacles to attendance. For example, employees are more likely to be able to come to work if the company can help them solve their transportation or day-care problems, or if their general health improves as a result of corporate-sponsored wellness programs. The important role of employee perceptions in this process was also discussed. That is, actual employee behavior is based largely on how employees interpret events around them. As such, an impediment to attendance to one employee (for example, a snow storm) might be seen as simply an inconvenience or even a challenge to another. To the extent that these obstacles—perceived and otherwise—can be reduced, motivated employees will be more likely to attend.

Combining the lessons of these three chapters leads us to the conclusion that employee attendance can be significantly enhanced to the extent that we can increase both the motivation to attend and the ability to attend. That is, by working on both sides of the problem, the likelihood of success is increased. Another conclusion to be reached from these three chapters is that managers can make a real difference in this area if they are so inclined. That is, instead of simply complaining about excessive employee absenteeism, an increasing number of companies are getting actively involved and approaching the problem systematically in an effort to discover long-term solutions that fit the particular culture and needs of the organization. Once the problem has been adequately diagnosed and once the most appropriate resolution strategies have been identified, managers are in a position to move in a constructive fashion.

The final question that should be addressed is where we go from here. However we look at it, the study of employee absenteeism has made significant progress in the last several years. It has gone from a topic that researchers looked at only casually as an analog of turnover (Porter and Steers, 1973) to a topic of importance in its own right (Goodman and Atkin, 1984a; Johns and Nicholson, 1982; Nicholson, 1977; Steers and Rhodes, 1978). Serious model development has emerged and, as noted above, numerous implications have been suggested for managers seriously interested in problem-solving. However, it would be a mistake to assume that our work is now done. More remains to be learned if we are to continue to assist managers with the difficult task of ensuring active employee participation in the workplace. Toward this end, several issues can be identified that comprise a future agenda for research on absenteeism (*see also:* Goodman and Atkin, 1984a; Steers and Rhodes, 1984).

First and perhaps foremost, we need more model testing under realistic field conditions. It can be argued that one of the benefits derived from the publication of such absence models as that proposed by Steers and Rhodes in 1978 was that it stimulated several useful attempts to test the model in different types of work organizations (see discussion in Chapter 3). These findings, combined with additional theoretical work, pointed to a number of suggestions for improved model development. In fact, the diagnostic model suggested in Chapter 3 is a direct result of these combined efforts. Even so, although progress has been made, this developmental process must continue. It would be helpful to see additional efforts both on model development and on model testing. In these efforts, it would be particularly helpful to see comparative and comprehensive studies using an adequate array of study variables and testing hypotheses on multiple samples. In this way, numerous potential errors of both measurement and interpretation can be avoided or at least minimized.

Beyond model development and testing, more work is called for in measuring the costs of absenteeism to organizations. As noted in Chapter 2, methods do exist for such calculations, but they are admittedly crude. For example, current methods, in only treating costs associated with absence, fail to consider that there may be a minimum level of absence at which even greater costs are associated with attendance as in the case where employees attend work when they are ill (see Chapter 1). If organizations see absence reduction as an important ingredient in organizational effectiveness and industrial competitiveness, then it becomes increasingly vital that accurate cost figures be established. Here is an area in which organizational researchers can work with accountants to pool their expertise for problem-solving.

Once more accurate cost data can be developed, managers can more precisely establish the costs of absences and the savings from absence reduction programs.

Third, we believe that more research is necessary on the social psychology of absence. That is, as noted in Chapter 1, absence has different meanings to different people and to different subgroups of people. Although some managers might see such behavior as a challenge to managerial authority, some employees might see it as either a simple necessity (in the case of a sick child at home) or as part of the compensation program ("If I don't take it I'll lose it."). Clearly, these different interpretations of the behavior color how we respond, either as managers or as employees. They determine to a large extent how all parties involved come to view the psychological contract between employees and organizations, and they have a direct impact on the emerging absence culture. Although much progress has been made on this topic (see, for example, Johns and Nicholson, 1982), more work is necessary to deepen our awareness of how perceptions and interpretative biases influence decisions about workplace participation. In this regard, a qualitative approach in which the researcher asks subjects direct questions about their absence behavior would be an appropriate research strategy (see Johns, 1984).

Fourth, related to the preceding issue is the need for research on how absence cultures are developed and on the influence of absence cultures on individual behavior. As we pointed out in Chapter 3, the literature on absence culture is largely conceptual and without significant research support. Research methodologies focusing on individual-level analyses would be inappropriate for examining absence cultures. Rather, Johns (1984) suggests aggregating organizational units according to the variance in absence (indicating more or less salient absence cultures). After this, variables could be identified that distinguish between high- and low-variance units. Finally, it might be possible to predict absence levels in different organizational units.

Fifth, additional work would be useful on the topic of the consequences of absence. Again, much useful work has emerged of late (for example, Goodman and Atkin, 1984b; Mowday, Porter, and Steers, 1982), but more empirically verifiable work would benefit the field. A good example of such work can be seen in the recent work of Goodman and Garber (1988) focusing on absenteeism and its consequences in coal mines. Such efforts should be extended to include more variables associated with potential consequences, as well as more diverse

samples. Furthermore, it would be helpful to establish which consequences are more universal in nature and which are confined to a
particular industry or work population.

Finally, we have seen considerable progress on designing
mechanisms to enhance employees' motivation and capacity to come
to work. We have classified these various techniques into three general
managerial strategies for absence reduction: 1) developing suitable
absence control policies; 2) creating attendance-oriented cultures; and
3) improving employees' ability to attend. A number of examples were
provided concerning the effectiveness of these techniques depending
upon the specific situation facing managers, but for the most part
*research support for the effectiveness of these strategies in reducing
absence is slight or nonexistent.* Often the strategies were proposed
based on correlational rather than experimental support (for example,
smokers are absent more than nonsmokers). With regard to absence
control policies, eleven of thirteen strategies discussed have been
empirically examined in no more than one study each. Strategies
receiving the greatest research attention were employee bonuses and
the lottery or poker system. Similarly, with the exception of redesigning
work, programs suggested to create an attendance-oriented culture
have little or no evaluational research support. Finally, of the strategies
aimed at improving ability to attend, only the effects of physical fitness
programs, employee assistance programs, and alternative work
schedules on absence have been evaluated to any great extent. In the
few cases where a number of research studies did exist, these studies
were often not well-controlled.

Clearly, then, as programs designed to reduce absence are implemented, it is critical that rigorous evaluation of their effectiveness is
undertaken. Moreover, it would be helpful to see more comprehensive
analyses comparing the relative effectiveness of several techniques in
the same study. For example, is sick child-care more cost effective in
reducing absences than a comprehensive company-sponsored day care
center? Is it more effective to spend one's energies on developing an
attendance-oriented culture or on enforcing absence control policies?
In view of limited corporate resources, choices presumably have to be
made concerning how best to use these resources to maximize results.
How many strategies can be realistically implemented simultaneously,
and which strategies should be attempted first? In point of fact, we
know little about how to make such choices, or even whether it is

possible to make such choices. This dilemma represents a fruitful area for further work by interested scholars and managers.

In conclusion, as we look back on research on employee absenteeism over the past decade, it must be concluded that significant progress has been made, both theoretically and empirically, yet there is more work that needs to be done. When the research on this topic was first reviewed in 1978, only 104 studies of typically poor quality were found (Steers and Rhodes, 1978). Many of these studies incorporated absence measures into larger research projects where the focus was on some other outcome variable (for example, performance, turnover). Absence measures were often ill-defined or poorly specified, and research designs left much to be desired. In concluding their review, Steers and Rhodes (p. 392) noted that "investigators of employee absenteeism have typically examined bivariate correlations between a set of variables and subsequent absenteeism. Little in the way of comprehensive theory building can be found. . . ." Since then, however, considerable progress has been made on all fronts. The number of absence studies—including studies focusing specifically on absenteeism—has escalated dramatically. Moreover, the quality of these studies has increased, with better specification of central variables and more sophisticated techniques of data analysis. Better theoretical development can also be found. In short, it must be concluded that we have made much progress on this topic. Our hope for the future is that this progress will continue in such a way that it benefits both researchers and managers in the field. In this way, we hope to see a continuation of the "town and gown" partnership that typifies good research in the behavioral sciences.

References

Aanonsen, A. (1964). *Shift Work and Health*. Oslo: Norwegian Monographs on Medical Science.

Adams, J. C. (1965). "Injustice in Social Exchange." In L. Berkowitz (ed.), *Advances in Experimental Social Psychology* (Vol. 2). New York: Academic Press.

Alander, R., and Campbell, T. (1975). "An Evaluative Study of an Alcohol and Drug Recovery Program: A Case Study of the Oldsmobile Experience." *Human Resource Management, 14*(1), pp. 14–18.

Alderman, M., and Davis, T. (1976). "Hypertension Control at the Worksite." *Journal of Occupational Medicine, 18*, pp. 793–796.

"Alfasud, Italy's Well-Intended Industrial Disaster." (March 10, 1979). *The Economist*, p. 81.

Allen, S. G. (1981). "An Empirical Model of Work Attendance." *The Review of Economics and Statistics, 63*, pp. 77–87.

———. (1984). "Trade Unions, Absenteeism, and Exit-Voice." *Industrial and Labor Relations Review, 37*, pp. 331–345.

Argyle, M. (1972). *The Social Psychology of Work*. Harmondsworth: Penguin.

Arsenault, A., and Dolan, S. (1983). "The Role of Personality, Occupation and Organization in Understanding the Relationship between Job Stress, Performance, and Absenteeism." *Journal of Occupational Psychology, 56,* pp. 227–240.

Arvey, R. D., and Ivancevich, J. M. (1980). "Punishment in Organizations: A Review, Propositions, and Research Suggestions." *Academy of Management Review, 5,* pp. 123–132.

Asma, F. E., Eggert, R. L., and Hilker, R. R. J. (1971). "Long-term Experience with Rehabilitation of Alcoholic Employees." *Journal of Occupational Medicine, 13,* pp. 581–585.

Athanasou, J. A. (1975). "Sickness Absence and Smoking Behavior and Its Consequences: A Review." *Journal of Occupational Medicine, 17,* pp. 441–445.

Athanasou, J. A., Reid, C. C., and Ferguson, D. A. (1981). "Sickness Absence and Smoking." *Medical Journal of Australia, 1,* pp. 211–212.

Atkin, R. S., and Goodman, P. S. (1984). "Methods of Defining and Measuring Absenteeism." In P. S. Goodman and R. S. Atkin (eds.), *Absenteeism: New Approaches to Understanding, Measuring, and Managing Employee Absence,* pp. 47–109. San Francisco: Jossey-Bass.

Azevedo, R. E. (1974). "Scientists, Engineers, and the Job Search Process." *California Management Review, 17*(1), pp. 40–49.

Bandura, A. (1969). *Principles of Behavior Modification.* New York: Holt, Rinehart and Winston.

Bandura, A. (1982). Self-Efficacy Mechanism in Human Agency. *American Psychologist, 37,* pp. 122–147.

Baum, J. F. (1978). "Effectiveness of an Attendance Control Policy in Reducing Chronic Absenteeism." *Personnel Psychology, 31,* pp. 71–81.

Baum, J. F., and Menefee, M. L. (1979). "An Experimental Study of Operant Conditioning and Absenteeism." Paper presented at the Academy of Management meeting, Atlanta.

Baun, M. S., Bernacki, E. J., and Tsai, S. P. (1986). "A Preliminary Investigation: Effect of a Corporate Fitness Program on Absenteeism and Health Care Cost." *Journal of Occupational Medicine, 28,* pp. 18–22.

Behrend, H. (1959). "Voluntary Absence from Work." *International Labour Review, 79,* pp. 109–140.

Bernacki, E. J., and Baun, W. B. (1984). "The Relationship of Job Performance to Exercise Adherence in a Corporate Fitness Program." *Journal of Occupational Medicine, 26,* pp. 529–531.

Bhagat, R. S., McQuaid, S. J., Lindholm, H., and Segovis, J. (1985). "Total Life Stress: A Multimethod Validation of the Construct and Its Effect on Organizationally Valued Outcomes and Withdrawal Behaviors." *Journal of Applied Psychology, 70,* pp. 202–214.

Brandt, A. (1969). "Uber den Einfluss der Schichtarbeit auf den Gesundheitszustand und das Krankheitsgescheben der Werktatigen." In *Proceedings of an International Symposium on Night and Shift Work.* Stockholm: Studia Laboris et Salutis No. 4.

Brayfield, A., and Crockett, W. (1955). "Employee Attitudes and Employee Performance." *Psychological Bulletin, 52,* pp. 396–424.

Breaugh, J. A. (1981a). "Predicting Absenteeism from Prior Absenteeism and Work Attitudes." *Journal of Applied Psychology, 66,* pp. 555–560.

———. (1981b). "Relationships between Recruiting Sources and Employee Performance, Absenteeism, and Work Attitudes." *Academy of Management Journal, 24,* pp. 142–147.

———. (1983). "Realistic Job Previews: A Critical Appraisal and Future Research Directions." *Academy of Management Review, 8,* pp. 612–619.

Brecher, J. (August 22, 1983). "Taking Drugs on the Job." *Newsweek, 101*(8), pp. 52–60.

Brennan, A. J. J. (1983). "Worksite Health Promotion Can be Cost-Effective." *Personnel Administrator, 28*(4), pp. 39–42.

Brooke, P. P. (1986). "Beyond the Steers and Rhodes Model of Employee Attendance." *Academy of Management Review, 11,* pp. 345–361.

Brooke, P. P., Jr., and Price, J. L. (1989). "The Determinants of Employee Absenteeism: An Empirical Test of a Causal Model." *Journal of Occupational Psychology, 62,* pp. 1–19.

Brumback, C. J. (April–June, 1987). "EAPs – Bringing Health and Productivity to the Workplace." *Business, 37,* pp. 42–45.

Bruno, M. (September 2, 1985). "Day Care on the Job: Since 1982, Corporate Child-Care Centers Have Tripled." *Newsweek, 106,* pp. 59, 62.

Bureau of National Affairs (1981). *Personnel Policies Forum Survey No. 132.* Washington, D.C.: Bureau of National Affairs.

Bureau of National Affairs (1983). *Controlling Health Care Costs: Crisis in Employee Benefits.* Washington, D.C.: Bureau of National Affairs.

Burton, W. N., Eggum, P. R., and Keller, P. J. (1981). "'High-Cost' Employees in an Occupational Alcoholism Program: A Preliminary Report." *Journal of Occupational Medicine, 23*(4), pp. 259–262.

Burud, S. L., Collins, R. C., and Divine-Hawkins, P. (1983). "Employer-Supported Child Care: Everybody Benefits." *Children Today, 12*(3), pp. 2–7.

Buzzard, R. B., and Liddell, F. D. K. (1958). *Coalminers' Attendance at Work.* NCB Medical Service, Medical Research Memorandum No. 3.

Campion, M. A., and Thayer, P. W. (1985). "Development and Field Evaluation of an Interdisciplinary Measure of Job Design." *Journal of Applied Psychology, 70,* pp. 29–43.

———. (1987). "Job Design: Approaches, Outcomes, and Trade-Offs." *Organizational Dynamics, 15*(3), pp. 66–79.

Caplan, R. D., Cobb, S., French, J. R. P., Jr., Harrison, R. D., and Pinneau, S. R., Jr. (1975). *Job Demands and Worker Health: Main*

Effects and Occupational Differences. Washington, D.C.: U.S. Government Printing Office.

Carlson, J. G., and Hill, K. D. (1982). "The Effect of Gaming on Attendance and Attitude." *Personnel Psychology, 25,* pp. 63–73.

Carroll, S. J., and Nash, A. N. (1972). "Effectiveness of a Forced-Choice Reference Check." *Personnel Psychology, 25,* pp. 42–46.

Cascio, W. F. (1987). *Costing Human Resources: The Financial Impact of Behavior in Organizations.* Boston: PWS-Kent.

Chadwick-Jones, J. K., Brown, C.A., and Nicholson, N. (1973). "Absence from Work: Its Meaning, Measurement and Control." *International Review of Applied Psychology, 22,* pp. 137–156.

Chadwick-Jones, J. K., Brown, C. A., Nicholson, N., and Sheppard, C. (1971). "Absence Measures: Their Reliability and Stability in an Industrial Setting." *Personnel Psychology, 24,* pp. 463–470.

Chadwick-Jones, J. K., Nicholson, N., and Brown, C. (1982). *Social Psychology of Absenteeism.* New York: Praeger.

Chelius, J. R. (1981). "Understanding Absenteeism: The Potential Contribution of Economic Theory." *Journal of Business Research, 9,* pp. 409–418.

Cherns, A. (1976). "The Principles of Sociotechnical Design." *Human Relations, 29,* pp. 783–792.

Clegg, C. W. (1983). "Psychology of Employee Lateness, Absence, and Turnover: A Methodological Critique and an Empirical Study." *Journal of Applied Psychology, 68,* pp. 88–101.

Colligan, M. J., Frockt, I. J., and Tasto, D. L. (1979). "Frequency of Sickness Absence and Work-Site Clinic Visits among Nurses as a Function of Shift." *Applied Ergonomics, 10*(2), pp. 79–85.

Colquhoun, W. P. (1976). "Accidents, Injuries, and Shift Work." In P. Rentos and R. Shepard (eds.), *Shift Work and Health: A Symposium* (U.S. Department of Health, Education, and Welfare Publication No. NIOSH 76-203). Washington, D.C.: Government Printing Office.

Cummings, T. G. (1976). "Sociotechnical Systems: An Intervention Strategy." In W. W. Burke (ed.), *Current Issues and Strategies in Organization Development,* pp. 187–213. New York: Human Sciences Press.

Cummings, T. G., and Molloy, E. S. (1977). *Improving Productivity and the Quality of Work Life.* New York: Praeger.

Cummings, T. G., Molloy, E. S., and Glen, R. (1977). "A Methodological Critique of Fifty-Eight Selected Work Experiments." *Human Relations, 30,* pp. 675–708.

Dalton, D. R., and Perry, J. L. (1981). "Absenteeism and the Collective Bargaining Agreement: An Empirical Test." *Academy of Management Journal, 24,* pp. 425–431.

Davis, L. E. (June 1977). "Job Design: Overview and Future Direction." *Journal of Contemporary Business,* pp. 85–102.

Decker, P. J., and Cornelius, E. T. (1979). "A Note on Recruiting Sources and Job Survival Rates." *Journal of Applied Psychology, 64,* pp. 463–464.

Deitsch, C. R., and Dilts, D. A. (1981). "To Cut Casual Absenteeism: Tie Benefits to Hours Worked." *Compensation Review, 13*(1), pp. 41–46.

Denerley, R. A. (1952). "Some Effects of Paid Sick Leave on Sickness Absence." *British Journal of Industrial Medicine, 9*(4), pp. 275–281.

Dickinson, K. (1975). "Child Care." In G. J. Duncan and J. N. Morgan (eds.), *Five Thousand Families — Patterns of Economic Progress* (Vol. 3). Ann Arbor: The Institute for Social Research, The University of Michigan.

Dickman, F., and Emener, W. G. (1982). "Employee Assistance Programs: Basic Concepts, Attributes and an Evaluation." *Personnel Administrator, 27*(8), pp. 55–62.

Dittrich, J. E., and Carrell, M. R. (1979). "Organizational Equity Perceptions, Employee Job Satisfaction, and Departmental Absence and Turnover Rates." *Organizational Behavior and Human Performance, 24,* pp. 29–40.

Dolan, S. L. (1983). "Working Mothers' Absenteeism: Does Workplace Day Care Make a Difference?" *Proceedings of the Eastern Academy of Management,* pp. 48–51.

Donoghue, S. (1977). "The Correlation between Physical Fitness, Absenteeism, and Work Performance." *Canadian Journal of Public Health, 68,* pp. 201–203.

Driver, R. W., and Ratliff, R. A. (1982). "Employers' Perceptions of Benefits Accrued from Physical Fitness Programs." *Personnel Administrator, 27*(8), pp. 21–26.

Duncan, G. J., and Coe, R. D. (July 1978). "Absenteeism, Statistical Discrimination and the Wages of Men and Women." Ann Arbor: University of Michigan Survey Research Center, Unpublished Paper.

Dunn, L. F., and Youngblood, S. A. (1986). "Absenteeism as a Mechanism for Approaching an Optimal Labor Market Equilibrium: An Empirical Study." *The Review of Economics and Statistics, 68,* pp. 668–674.

Dunne, J. A. (1977). "Evaluating the New York City Police Department Counseling Unit." In C. J. Schramm (ed.), *Alcoholism and Its Treatment in Industry.* Baltimore: Johns Hopkins University Press, pp. 91–108.

Durand, V. M. (1983). "Behavioral Ecology of a Staff Incentive Program: Effects on Absenteeism and Resident Disruptive Behavior." *Behavior Modification, 7,* pp. 165–181.

EAP, Inc. (1984). *EAP Supervisor Training Workbook.* Indianapolis: EAP, Inc.

Edwards, D., Bucky, S., Coben, P., Fichman, S., and Berry, N. H. (1977). "Primary and Secondary Benefits from Treatment for Alcoholism." *American Journal of Psychiatry, 134*(6), pp. 682–683.

Edwards, P., and Scullion, H. (July 1979). "Does Sick Pay Encourage Absenteeism?" *Personnel Management,* pp. 32–35.

Emery, F. E. (1978). "On Socio-Technical Systems." In W. A. Pasmore and J. J. Sherwood (eds.), *Sociotechnical Systems: A Sourcebook,* pp. 43–57. LaJolla: University Associates.

Emery, F. E., and Trist, E. L. (1978). "Analytical Model for Sociotechnical Systems." In W. A. Pasmore and J. J. Sherwood (eds.), *Sociotechnical Systems: A Sourcebook*, pp. 120–131. La Jolla: University Associates.

English, C. W. (December 5, 1983). "Getting Tough on Work Abuse of Drugs, Alcohol." *U.S. News and World Report, 95*(23), p. 85.

Falkenberg, L. E. (1987). "Employee Fitness Programs: Their Impact on the Employee and the Organization." *Academy of Management Review, 12,* pp. 511–522.

Farrell, D., and Stamm, C. L. (1988). "Meta-Analysis of the Correlates of Employee Absence." *Human Relations, 41,* pp. 211–227.

Ferguson, D. (1973). "Smoking, Drinking and Non-Narcotic Analgesic Habits in an Occupational Group." *Medical Journal of Australia, 1,* pp. 1271–1274.

Fichman, M. (1988). "Motivational Consequences of Absence and Attendance: Proportional Hazard Estimation of a Dynamic Motivation Model." *Journal of Applied Psychology, 73,* pp. 119–134.

Fielding, J. E. (1982). "Effectiveness of Employee Health Improvement Programs." *Journal of Occupational Medicine, 24,* pp. 907–916.

———. (October 5, 1987). "Ingredients of Successful Health Promotion Programs." *Barron's,* pp. 58–59.

Fitzgibbons, D., and Moch, M. (1980). "Employee Absenteeism: A Multivariate Analysis with Replication." *Organizational Behavior and Human Performance, 26,* pp. 349–372.

Ford, J. E. (1981). "A Simple Punishment Procedure for Controlling Employee Absenteeism." *Journal of Organizational Behavior Management, 3*(2), pp. 71–79.

Ford, R. N. (1969). *Motivation Through the Work Itself.* New York: American Management Association.

Frayne, C. A., and Latham, G. P. (1987). "Application of Social Learning Theory to Employee Self-Management of Attendance." *Journal of Applied Psychology, 72,* pp. 387–392.

Frechette, H. M. (1981). "An Investigation of the Utility of Steers and Rhodes Process Model of Attendance Behavior." Paper presented at the 41st Annual Meeting of the Academy of Management, San Diego.

Frederiksen, L. W., and Lovett, S. B. (1980). "Inside Organizational Behavior Management: Perspectives on an Emerging Field." *Journal of Organizational Behavior Management, 2,* pp. 193–203.

Freedberg, E. J., and Johnston, W. E. (1981). "The Relationship between Alcoholism Treatment Outcome in Terms of Drinking and Various Patient Characteristics." *Journal of Occupational Medicine, 23*(1), pp. 30–34.

Fried, Y., and Ferris, G. R. (1987). "The Validity of the Job Characteristics Model: A Review and Meta-Analysis." *Personnel Psychology, 40,* pp. 287–322.

Friedman, D. E. (September 1980). "Child Care in the 80s — Reaching Out to Business and Labor." *Child Care Information Exchange, 15,* pp. 7–12.

———. (1985). *Corporate Financial Assistance for Child Care* (Research Bulletin No. 177). New York: The Conference Board Work and Family Information Center.

———. (1986). "Child Care for Employees' Kids." *Harvard Business Review, 86*(2), pp. 28–34.

———. (1987). *Family-Supportive Policies: The Corporate Decision-Making Process.* New York: The Conference Board Work and Family Information Center.

Galloway, D., Panckhurst, F., Boswell, K., Boswell, C., and Green, K. (1984). "Mental Health, Absences from Work, Stress and Satisfaction in a Sample of New Zealand Primary School Teachers." *Australian and New Zealand Journal of Psychiatray, 18,* pp. 359–363.

Gandz, J., and Mikalachki, A. (1979). "Measuring Absenteeism." Working Paper Series No. 217, University of Western Ontario.

Ganster, D. C., Mayes, B. T., Sime, W. E., and Tharp, G. D. (1982). "Managing Organizational Stress: A Field Experiment." *Journal of Applied Psychology, 67,* pp. 533–542.

Gardner, J. M. (1970). "Effects of Reinforcement Conditions on Lateness and Absence among Institutional Personnel." *Ohio Research Quarterly, 3,* pp. 315–316.

Gary, A. L. (1971). "Industrial Absenteeism: An Evaluation of Three Methods of Treatment." *Personnel Journal, 50,* pp. 352–353.

Gaudet, F. J. (1963). *Solving the Problems of Employee Absence* (AMA Research Study 57). New York: American Management Association.

Gibson, R. O. (1966). "Toward a Conceptualization of Absence Behavior." *Administrative Sciences Quarterly, 11,* pp. 107–133.

Glass, G. V., Willson, V. L., and Gottman, J. M. (1975). *Design and Analysis of Time Series Experiments.* Boulder: Colorado Associated University Press.

Golembiewski, R. T., and Proehl, C. W., Jr. (1978). "A Survey of the Empirical Literature on Flexible Workhours: Character and Consequences of a Major Innovation." *Academy of Management Review, 3,* pp. 837–853.

Goodman, P., and Atkin, R. (1984a). *Absenteeism: New Approaches to Understanding, Measuring, and Managing Employee Absence.* San Francisco: Jossey-Bass.

———. (1984b). "Effects of Absenteeism on Individuals and Organizations." In P. S. Goodman and R. S. Atkin (eds.), *Absenteeism: New Approaches to Understanding, Measuring, and Managing Employee Absence,* pp. 276–321. San Francisco: Jossey-Bass.

Goodman, P., and Garber, S. (1988). "Absenteeism and Accidents in a Dangerous Environment: Empirical Analysis of Underground Coal Mines." *Journal of Applied Psychology, 73,* pp. 81–86.

Gordon, C., Emerson, R. A., and Pugh, D. S. (1959). "Patterns of Sickness Absence in a Railway Population." *British Journal of Industrial Medicine, 16,* pp. 230–244.

Gowler, D. (1969). "Determinants of the Supply of Labour to the Firm." *Journal of Management Studies, 6,* pp. 73–95.

Greene, J. A. (1974). "Restructuring Staff Time: The 8-Day Week." *Hospital and Community Psychiatry, 25,* pp. 733–735.

Griffin, R. W. (1982). *Task Design: An Integrative Approach.* Glenview, Ill.: Scott, Foresman.

Grimaldi, P. L., and Simonds, R. H. (1975). *Safety Management.* Homewood, Ill.: Irwin.

Grove, B. A. (1968). "Attendance Reward Plan Pays." *Personnel Journal, 47,* pp. 119–120.

Gupta, N., and Beehr, T. A. (1979). "Job Stress and Employee Behavior." *Organizational Behavior and Human Performance, 23,* pp. 373–387.

Hackett, R. D. (1988). "Yet Another Look at the Relationship of Employee Absenteeism to Job Satisfaction." Hamilton, Canada: Faculty of Business Research and Working Paper Series #290.

Hackett, R. D., and Guion, R. M. (1985). "A Reevaluation of the Absenteeism-Job Satisfaction Relationship." *Organizational Behavior and Human Decision Processes, 35,* pp. 340–381.

Hackman, J. R., and Oldham, G. R. (1975). "Development of the Job Diagnostic Survey." *Journal of Applied Psychology, 60,* pp. 159–170.

———. (1976). "Motivation through the Design of Work: Test of a Theory." *Organizational Behavior and Human Performance, 16,* pp. 250–279.

———. (1980). *Work Redesign.* Reading, MA: Addison-Wesley.

Hackman, J. R., Oldham, G. R., Janson, R., and Purdy, K. (1975). "A New Strategy for Job Enrichment." *California Management Review, 17*(4), pp. 57–71.

Hammer, T. H., Landau, J., and Stern, R. N. (1981). "Absenteeism When Workers Have a Voice: The Case of Employee Ownership." *Journal of Applied Psychology, 66,* pp. 561–573.

Hamner, W. C. (1974). "Reinforcement Theory and Contingency Management in Organizational Settings." In H. L. Tosi and W. C. Hamner (eds.), *Organizational Behavior and Management: A Contingency Approach,* pp. 86–112. Chicago: St. Clair Press.

Harvey, B. H., and Luthans, F. (Summer 1979). "Flexitime: An Empirical Analysis of Its Real Meaning and Impact." *MSU Business Topics, 27,* pp. 31–36.

Harvey, B. H., Rogers, J. F., and Schultze, J. A. (1983). "Sick Pay vs Well Pay: An Analysis of the Impact of Rewarding Employees for Being on the Job." *Public Personnel Management Journal, 12,* pp. 218–224.

Herbst, P. (1962). *Autonomous Group Functioning.* London: Tavistock.

Herzberg, F. (1966). *Work and the Nature of Man.* Cleveland: World.

Hiatt, A. (November 1982). "Child Care: A Business Responsibility." *Industry Week, 215*(5), p. 13.

Higgins, C. W., and Philips, B. U. (1979). "How Company-Sponsored Fitness Programs Keep Employees on the Job." *Management Review, 68*(8), pp. 53–55.

Hill, J. M. M., and Trist, E. L. (1953). "A Consideration of Industrial Accidents as a Means of Withdrawal from the Work Situation." *Human Relations, 6,* pp. 357–380.

Hirayama, T. (1981). "Non-Smoking Wives of Heavy Smokers Have a Higher Risk of Lung Cancer: A Study from Japan." *The British Medical Journal, 282,* pp. 183–185.

Hofferth, S. L. (1979). "Day Care in the Next Decade: 1980–1990." *Journal of Marriage and the Family, 41,* pp. 649–657.

Ilgen, D., and Hollenback, J. H. (1977). "The Role of Job Satisfaction in Absence Behavior." *Organizational Behavior and Human Performance, 19,* pp. 148–161.

Ivancevich, J. M. (1974). "Effects of the Shorter Workweek on Selected Satisfaction and Performance Measures." *Journal of Applied Psychology, 59,* pp. 717–721.

———. (1986). "Life Events and Hassles as Predictors of Health Symptoms, Job Performance, and Absenteeism." *Journal of Occupational Behaviour, 7,* pp. 39–51.

Ivancevich, J. M., and Lyon, H. L. (1977). "The Shortened Workweek: A Field Experiment." *Journal of Applied Psychology, 62,* pp. 34–37.

Jablonsky, S. F., and DeVries, D. L. (1972). "Operant Conditioning Principles Extrapolated to the Theory of Management." *Organizational Behavior and Human Performance, 7,* pp. 340–358.

Jackson, S. E. (1983). "Participation in Decision-Making as a Strategy for Reducing Job-Related Strain." *Journal of Applied Psychology, 68,* pp. 3–19.

Jamal, M. (1981). "Shift Work Related to Job Attitudes, Social Participation and Withdrawal Behavior: A Study of Nurses and Industrial Workers." *Personnel Psychology, 34,* pp. 535–547.

Johns, G. (1978). "Attitudinal and Nonattitudinal Predictors of Two Forms of Absence from Work." *Organizational Behavior and Human Performance, 22,* pp. 431–444.

———. (1984). "Unresolved Issues in the Study and Management of Absence from Work." In P. S. Goodman and R. S. Atkin (eds.), *Absenteeism: New Approaches to Understanding, Measuring, and Managing Employee Absence,* pp. 360–390. San Francisco: Jossey-Bass.

Johns, G., and Nicholson, N. (1982). "The Meaning of Absence: New Strategies for Theory and Research." In B. M. Staw and L. L. Cummings (eds.), *Research in Organizational Behavior* (Vol. 4). Greenwich, CT: JAI.

Johnston, J. M. (1972). "Punishment of Human Behavior." *American Psychologist, 27,* pp. 1033–1054.

Jordan, F. C. (September 1973). "A Fair System of Time Off the Job: Combine Sick Days, Vacation Days, and Holidays into Paid Days." *Modern Hospital, 5,* pp. 49–52.

Kamerman, S. B. (1983). "Child-Care Services: A National Picture." *Monthly Labor Review, 106*(12), pp. 35–39.

Katzell, R. A., Bienstock, P., and Faerstein, P. H. (1977). *A Guide to Worker Productivity Experiments in the United States 1971–1975.* New York: University Press.

Kazdin, A. E. (1975). *Behavior Modification in Applied Settings.* Homewood, Ill.: Dorsey, 1975.

Keller, R. T. (1983). "Predicting Absenteeism from Prior Absenteeism, Attitudinal Factors, and Nonattitudinal Factors." *Journal of Applied Psychology, 68,* pp. 536–540.

Kempen, R. W., and Hall, R. V. (1977). "Reduction of Industrial Absenteeism: Results of a Behavioral Approach." *Journal of Organizational Behavior Management, 1,* pp. 1–21.

Kent, D. C., Schram, M., and Cenci, L. (1982). "Smoking in the Workplace: A Review of Human and Operating Costs." *Personnel Administrator, 27*(8), pp. 29, 21–33, 83.

Kent, H. M., Malott, R. W., and Greening, M. (1977). "Improving Attendance at Work in a Volunteer Food Cooperative with a Token Economy." *Journal of Organizational Behavior Management, 1,* pp. 89–98.

Kim, J. S., and Campagna, A. F. (1981). "Effects of Flexitime on Employee Attendance and Performance: A Field Experiment." *Academy of Management Journal, 24,* pp. 729–741.

Klein, B. W. (1986). "Missed Work and Lost Hours, May 1985." *Monthly Labor Review, 109*(11), pp. 26–30.

Klesges, R. C., Cigrang, J., and Glasgow, R. E. (1987). "Work Site Smoking Modification Programs: A State-of-the-Art Review and Directions for Future Research." *Current Psychological Research and Reviews, 6*(1), pp. 26–56.

Klesges, R. C., and Glasgow, R. E. (1986). "Smoking Modification in the Worksite." In M. F. Cataldo and T. J. Coates (eds.), *Health and Industry: A Behavioral Medicine Perspective.* New York: Wiley Interscience.

Kolodny, H. F., and Dresner, B. (1986). "Linking Arrangements and New Work Designs." *Organizational Dynamics, 14*(3), pp. 33–51.

Kondrasuk, J. N. (1980). "Company Physical Fitness Programs: Salvation or Fad?" *Personnel Administrator, 25*(22), pp. 47–50, 60.

Kopelman, R. E. (1985). "Job Redesign and Productivity: A Review of the Evidence." *National Productivity Review, 4,* pp. 237–255.

Kopelman, R. E., and Schneller, G. O. (1981). "A Mixed-Consequence System for Reducing Overtime and Unscheduled Absence." *Journal of Organizational Behavior Management, 3*(1), pp. 17–28.

Kopelman, R. E., Schneller, G. O., IV, and Silver, J. J., Jr. (1981). "Parkinson's Law and Absenteeism: A Program to Rein in Sick Leave Costs." *Personnel Administrator, 26*(5), pp. 57–64.

Krausz, M., and Freibach, N. (1983). "Effects of Flexible Working Time for Employed Women upon Satisfaction, Strains, and Absenteeism." *Journal of Occupational Psychology, 56,* pp. 155–159.

Krug, D. N., Palmour, V. E., and Bellassai, M. C. (1972). *Evaluation of the Office of Economic Opportunity Child Development Center.* Washington, D.C.: U.S. Government Printing Office.

Kuzmits, F. E. (1979). "How Much Is Absenteeism Costing Your Organization?" *Personnel Administrator, 24*(6), pp. 29–33.

———. (1981). "No Fault: A New Strategy for Absenteeism Control." *Personnel Journal, 60,* pp. 387–390.

La Fleur, E. K., and Newsom, W. B. (1988). "Opportunities for Child Care." *Personnel Administrator, 33*(6), pp. 146–154.

Latham, G. P., and Frayne, C. A. (1989). "Self-Management Training for Increasing Job Attendance." *Journal of Applied Psychology, 74,* pp. 411–416.

Latham, G. P., and Napier, N. K. (1984). "Practical Ways to Increase Employee Attendance." In P. S. Goodman, R. S. Atkin, and Associates (eds.), *Absenteeism: New Approaches to Understanding, Measuring, and Managing Employee Absence,* pp. 322–359. San Francisco: Jossey-Bass.

Latham, G. P., and Saari, L. M. (1979). "The Application of Social Learning Theory to Training Supervisors through Behavioral Modeling." *Journal of Applied Psychology, 64,* pp. 239–246.

Lawler, E. E., III (1986). *High-Involvement Management.* San Francisco: Jossey-Bass.

Lawler, E. E., III, and Hackman, J. R. (1969). "Impact of Employee Participation in the Development of Pay Incentive Plans: A Field Experiment." *Journal of Applied Psychology, 53,* pp. 467–471.

Lawler, E. E., III, and Porter, L. W. (1967). "The Effect of Performance on Job Satisfaction." *Industrial Relations, 7,* pp. 20–28.

Lee, T. W. (1989). "The Antecedents and Prediction of Employee Attendance." *Journal of Business Issues, 17*(2), pp. 17–22.

Leigh, J. P. (1985). "The Effects of Unemployment and the Business Cycle on Absenteeism." *Journal of Economics and Business, 37,* pp. 159–170.

LeRoux, M. (1982). "Employers Finding Out Helping Workers Care for Children Pays Off." *Business Insurance, 16*(25), pp. 3, 10.

LeRoux, R. (1982). "Center Provides Haven for Recuperating Kids." *Business Insurance, 16*(25), p. 14.

"Linking Employee Fitness Programs to Lower Medical Costs and Absenteeism." *Monthly Labor Review, 110*(11), pp. 27–28.

Lofquist, L. H., and Dawis, R. V. (1969). *Adjustment to Work.* New York: Appleton-Century-Crofts.

Luthans, F., and Kreitner, R. (1974). "The Management of Behavioral Contingencies." *Personnel, 51*(4), pp. 7–16.

———. (1975). *Organizational Behavior Modification.* Glenview, Ill.: Scott Foresman.

Luthans, F., and Martinko, M. (Fall 1976). "An Organizational Behavior Modification Analysis of Absenteeism." *Human Resource Management, 15,* pp. 11–18.

Macy, B. A., and Mirvis, P. H. (1976). "A Methodology for Assessment of Quality of Work Life and Organizational Effectiveness in Behavioral-Economic Terms." *Administrative Science Quarterly, 21,* pp. 212–226.

Majchrzak, A. (1987). Effects of Management Policies on Unauthorized Absence Behavior. *Journal of Applied Behavioral Science, 23,* pp. 501–523.

Markham, S. E. (1985). "An Investigation of the Relationship between Unemployment and Absenteeism: A Multi-level Approach." *Academy of Management Journal, 28,* pp. 228–234.

Markham, S. E., Dansereau, F., Jr., and Alutto, J. A. (1982). "On the Use of Shift as an Independent Variable in Absenteeism Research." *Journal of Occupational Psychology, 55,* pp. 225–231.

Martin, J. (1971). "Some Aspects of Absence in a Light Engineering Factor." *Occupational Psychology, 45,* pp. 77–91.

Masi, D. A., and Teems, L. A. (1983). "Employee Counseling Services Evaluation System: Design, Issues, and Conclusions." *Evaluation and Program Planning, 6*(1), pp. 1–6.

Maxey, C., Roy, D. P., and Kerr, S. (1982). *A Study of Executive Heart Health Programs in Selected Companies.* Los Angeles: American Heart Association.

McKendrick, J. E. (1988). "Smoking Policies Take Off." *Management World, 17*(1), pp. 12–14.

McShane, S. L. (1984). "Job Satisfaction and Absenteeism: A Meta-Analytic Re-Examination." *Canadian Journal of Administrative Sciences, 1,* pp. 61–77.

Mellor, E. F. (1986). "Shift Work and Flexitime: How Prevalent Are They?" *Monthly Labor Review, 109*(11), pp. 14–21.

Milkovich, G. T., and Gomez, L. R. (1976). "Day Care and Selected Employee Work Behaviors." *Academy of Management Journal, 19,* pp. 111–115.

Miller, L. M. (1978). *Behavior Management: The New Science of Managing People at Work.* New York: Wiley.

Miller, T. I. (1984). "The Effects of Employer-Sponsored Child Care on Employee Absenteeism, Turnover, Productivity, Recruitment or Job Satisfaction: What is Claimed and What is Known." *Personnel Psychology, 37,* pp. 277–289.

Mobley, W. H. (1982). "Some Unanswered Questions in Turnover and Withdrawal Research." *Academy of Management Review, 7,* pp. 111–116.

Morgan, L. G., and Herman, J. B. (1976). "Perceived Consequences of Absenteeism." *Journal of Applied Psychology, 61,* pp. 738–742.

Mosel, J. N., and Goheen, H. W. (1959). "The Employment Recommendation Questionnaire: III. Validity of Different Types of References." *Personnel Psychology, 12,* pp. 469–477.

Mowday, R. T., Porter, L. W., and Steers, R. M. (1982). *Employee-Organization Linkages: The Psychology of Commitment, Absenteeism, and Turnover.* New York: Academic Press.

Murphy, L. R. (1984a). "Occupational Stress Management: A Review and Appraisal." *Journal of Occupational Psychology, 57,* pp. 1–15.

———. (1984b). "Stress Management in Highway Maintenance Workers." *Journal of Occupational Medicine, 26,* pp. 436–442.

———. (1986). "A Review of Organizational Stress Management Research: Methodological Considerations." *Journal of Organizational Behavior Management, 8,* pp. 215–227.

Narayanan, V. K., and Nath, R. (1982). "A Field Test of Some Attitudinal and Behavioral Consequences of Flexitime." *Journal of Applied Psychology, 67,* pp. 214–218.

Naus, D. M. A., Engler, V., Hetychova, M., and Vavreckova, O. (1966). "Work Injuries and Smoking." *Industrial Medicine and Surgery, 35,* pp. 880–881.

Newman, J. E. (1974). "Predicting Absenteeism and Turnover." *Journal of Applied Psychology, 59,* pp. 610–615.

Newstrom, J. W., and Pierce, J. L. (1979). "Alternative Work Schedules: The State of the Art." *Personnel Administrator, 24*(10), pp. 19–23.

Nicholson, N. (1976). "Management Sanctions and Absence Control." *Human Relations, 29,* pp. 139–151.

———. (1977). "Absence Behaviour and Attendance Motivation: A Conceptual Synthesis." *Journal of Management Studies, 14,* pp. 231–252.

Nicholson, N., and Goodge, P. M. (1976). "The Influence of Social, Organizational and Biographical Factors on Female Absence." *Journal of Management Studies, 13,* pp. 234–254.

Nicholson, N., Jackson, P., and Howes, G. (1978). "Shiftwork and Absence: An Analysis of Temporal Trends." *Journal of Occupational Psychology, 51,* pp. 127–137.

Nicholson, N., and Johns, G. (1985). "The Absence Culture and the Psychological Contract — Who's in Control of Absence?" *Academy of Management Review, 10,* pp. 397–407.

"No Smoking: A Profitable Policy." (1982). *Small Business Report, 7*(8), pp. 18–20.

Nollen, S. (1979). "Does Flexitime Improve Productivity?" *Harvard Business Review, 57*(5), pp. 16–18.

Nord, W. R. (1969). "Beyond the Teaching Machine: The Neglected Area of Operant Conditioning in the Theory and Practice of Management." *Organizational Behavior and Human Performance, 4,* pp. 375–401.

————. (1970). "Improving Attendance through Rewards." *Personnel Administration, 33*(6), pp. 37–41.

Nord, W. R., and Costigan, R. (1973). "Worker Adjustment to the Four-Day Week: A Longitudinal Study." *Journal of Applied Psychology, 58,* pp. 60–66.

Norris, E. (November 16, 1981). "Alcohol: Companies Are Learning It Pays to Help Workers Beat the Bottle. *Business Insurance, 15,* pp. 1, 53–54.

Orpen, C. (1978). "Effects of Bonuses for Attendance on the Absenteeism of Industrial Workers." *Journal of Organizational Behavior Management, 1,* pp. 118–124.

Panyan, S. W., and McGregor, M. (1976). "How to Implement a Proactive Incentive Plan: A Field Study." *Personnel Journal, 55,* pp. 460–462.

Paringer, L. (1983). "Women and Absenteeism: Health or Economics?" *The American Economic Review, 73*(2), pp. 123–127.

Parke, R. D. (1972). "Some Effects of Punishment on Children's Behavior." In W. W. Hartup (ed.), *The Young Child: Reviews of Research* (Vol. 2). Washington, D.C.: National Association for the Education of Young Children.

Parkes, K. R. (1983). "Smoking as a Moderator of the Relationship between Affective State and Absence from Work." *Journal of Applied Psychology, 68,* pp. 698–708.

———. (1987). "Relative Weight, Smoking, and Mental Health as Predictors of Sickness and Absences from Work." *Journal of Applied Psychology, 72,* pp. 275–286.

Pasmore, W., Francis, C., Haldeman, J., and Shani, A. (1982). "Sociotechnical Systems: A North American Reflection on Empirical Studies of the Seventies." *Human Relations, 35,* pp. 1179–1204.

Patchen, M. (1960). "Absence and Employee Feelings about Fair Treatment." *Personnel Psychology, 13,* pp. 349–360.

Pedalino, E., and Gamboa, V. V. (1974). "Behavior Modification and Absenteeism: Intervention in One Industrial Setting." *Journal of Applied Psychology, 59,* pp. 694–698.

Perry, K. S. (1978). *Survey and Analysis of Employer-Sponsored Day Care in the U.S.* Dissertation, University of Wisconsin, Madison. University Microfilms No. 79-05048.

———. (1982). *Employers and Child Care: Establishing Services through the Workplace.* (Pamphlet #23). Washington, D.C.: Women's Bureau.

Petersen, D. J. (1980). "Flexitime in the United States: The Lessons of Experience." *Personnel, 57*(1), pp. 21–31.

Pocock, S. J. (1973). "Daily Variations in Sickness Absence." *Applied Statistics, 22,* pp. 375–392.

Pocock, S. J., Sergean, R., and Taylor, P. J. (1972). "Absence of Continuous Three-Shift Workers." *Occupational Psychology, 46,* pp. 7–13.

Popp, P. O., and Belohlav, J. A. (1982). "Absenteeism in a Low Status Work Environment." *Academy of Management Journal, 25,* pp. 677–683.

Porter, L. W., and Lawler, E. E. (1968). *Managerial Attitudes and Performance.* Homewood, Ill.: Dorsey Press.

Porter, L. W., and Steers, R. M. (1973). "Organizational, Work, and Personal Factors in Employee Turnover and Absenteeism." *Psychological Bulletin, 80,* pp. 151–176.

Premack, S. L., and Wanous, J. P. (1985). "A Meta-Analysis of Realistic Job Preview Experiments." *Journal of Applied Psychology, 70,* pp. 706–719.

Prentice-Hall (May 29, 1979). *Personnel Management: Policies and Practices.* Englewood Cliffs, N.J.: Prentice Hall.

Prentice-Hall Editorial Staff (1981). *Absenteeism and Lateness.* Englewood Cliffs, N.J.: Prentice-Hall.

Quayle, D. (1983). "American Productivity: The Devastating Effect of Alcoholism and Drug Abuse." *American Psychologist, 38*(4), pp. 454–458.

Reid, D. H., Schuh-Wear, C. L., and Brannon, M. E. (April 1978). "Use of a Group Contingency to Decrease Staff Absenteeism in a State Institution." *Behavior Modification, 21,* pp. 251–266.

"Ride Sharing Packs Them in and Saves Money." (March 5, 1984). *Industry Week, 220*(5), pp. 85–86, 88.

Riley, A. W., Fredericksen, L. W., and Winett, R. A. (1984). "Stress Management in the Workplace: A Time for Caution in Health Promotion." *Report to NIOSH on P.O. 84-1320.* Cincinnati, Ohio.

Robertson, D. E., Johnson, R. D., and Bethke, A. L. (1980). "Reducing Absenteeism with Fixed and Variable Interval Reinforcement." *Review of Business and Economic Research, 15,* pp. 73–82.

Robertson, G., and Humphreys, J. (1978). "Labour Turnover and Absenteeism in Selected Industries: Northwestern Ontario and Ontario." *Component Study Number 10, Northwestern Manpower Adjustment Study.* Toronto.

Robins, J., and Lloyd, M. (1983). "A Case Study Examining the Effectiveness and Cost of Incentive Programs to Reduce Staff Absenteeism in a Preschool." *Journal of Organizational Behavior Management, 5*(3-4), pp. 175–189.

Rodriguez, R. A. (1983). "How to Judge Your Day Care Options." *Personnel Administrator, 28*(8), pp. 41–44.

Rosen, H., and Turner, J. (1971). "Effectiveness of Two Orientation Approaches in Hard-Core Unemployed Turnover and Absenteeism." *Journal of Applied Psychology, 55,* pp. 296–301.

Rosenthal, R. (1979). "Arbitral Standards for Absenteeism Discharges." *Labor Law Journal, 30,* pp. 732–740.

Rosse, J. G., and Hulin, C. L. (1985). "Adaptation to Work: An Analysis of Employee Health, Withdrawal, and Change." *Organizational Behavior and Human Decision Processes, 36,* pp. 324–347.

Rosse, J. G., and Miller, H. E. (1984). "Relationship between Absenteeism and Other Employee Behaviors." In P. S. Goodman and R. S. Atkin (eds.), *Absenteeism: New Approaches to Understanding, Measuring, and Managing Absence,* pp. 194–228. San Francisco: Jossey-Bass.

Saltman, J. (1977). *Drinking on the Job: The $15-Billion Hangover* (Public Affairs Pamphlet No. 544). New York: Public Affairs Committee, Inc.

Scheflen, K. C., Lawler, E. E., III, and Hackman, J. R. (1971). "Long-Term Impact of Employee Participation in the Development of Pay Incentive Plans: A Field Experiment Revisited." *Journal of Applied Psychology, 55,* pp. 182–186.

Schein, E. H. (1985). *Organizational Culture and Leadership: A Dynamic View.* San Francisco: Jossey-Bass.

Schlotzhauer, D. L., and Rosse, J. G. (1985). "A Five-Year Study of a Positive Incentive Absence Control Program." *Personnel Psychology, 38,* pp. 575–585.

Schmitz, L. M., and Heneman, H. G., III (1980). "Do Positive Reinforcement Programs Reduce Employee Absenteeism?" *Personnel Administrator, 25*(9), pp. 87–93.

Schneller, G. O., IV, and Kopelman, R. E. (1983). "Using Incentives to Increase Absenteeism: A Plan That Backfired." *Compensation Review, 15*(2), pp. 40–45.

Scott, K. D., and Markham, S. (1982). "Absenteeism Control Methods: A Survey of Practices and Results." *Personnel Administrator, 27*(6), pp. 73–84.

———. (1983). "An Analysis of Absenteeism Cases Taken to Arbitration: 1975–1981." *The Arbitration Journal, 38*(3), pp. 61–70.

———. (1985). "An Examination of Conflicting Findings on the Relationship between Job Satisfaction and Absenteeism." *Academy of Management Journal, 28*, pp. 599–612.

Scott, K. D., Markham, S. E., and Robers, R. W. (1985). "Rewarding Good Attendance: A Comparative Study of Positive Ways to Reduce Absenteeism." *Personnel Administrator, 30*(8), pp. 72–83.

Seamonds, B. C. (1982). "Stress Factors and Their Effect on Absenteeism in a Corporate Employee Group." *Journal of Occupational Medicine, 24*, pp. 393–397.

———. (1983). "Extension of Research into Stress Factors and Their Effect on Illness Absenteeism." *Journal of Occupational Medicine, 25*, pp. 821–822.

Seatter, W. C. (1961). "More Effective Control of Absenteeism." *Personnel, 38*(5), pp. 16–29.

Segal, M., and Weinberger, D. B. (1977). "Turfing." *Operations Research, 25*(3), pp. 367–386.

Sergean, R., and Brierly, J. (1968). "Absence and Attendance under Non-Continuous Three-Shift Systems of Work." *Nature, 219,* p. 536.

Shepherd, R. D., and Walker, J. (1956). "Three-Shift Working and the Distribution of Absence." *Occupational Psychology, 30,* pp. 105–111.

Sherwood, J. J. (1988). "Creating Work Cultures with Competitive Advantage." *Organizational Dynamics, 16*(3), pp. 4–27.

"Sick Pay—Infectious." (June 3, 1978). *The Economist, 267,* p. 124.

Silva, D. B., Duncan, P. K., and Doudna, D. (1981). "The Effects of Attendance-Contingent Feedback and Praise on Attendance and Work Efficiency." *Journal of Organizational Behavioral Management, 3,* pp. 59–69.

Skinner, B. F. (1938). *The Behavior of Organisms*. New York: Appleton-Century-Crofts.

―――. (1953). *Science and Human Behavior*. New York: Macmillan.

―――. (1954). "The Science of Learning and the Art of Teaching." *Harvard Educational Review, 24*, pp. 86–97.

Smith, F. J. (1977). "Work Attitudes as Predictors of Specific Day Attendance." *Journal of Applied Psychology, 62*, pp. 16–18.

Smith, M. J., Colligan, M. J., and Tasto, D. L. (1982). "Health and Safety Consequences of Shift Work in the Food Processing Industry." *Ergonomics, 25*(2), pp. 133–144.

Sonnenstuhl, W. J., and O'Donnell, J. E. (1980). "EAPs: The Why's and How's of Planning Them." *Personnel Administrator, 25*(11), pp. 35–38.

Staw, B. M., and Oldham, G. R. (1978). "Reconsidering Our Dependent Variables: A Critique and Empirical Study." *Academy of Management Journal, 21*, pp. 539–559.

Steers, R. M., and Rhodes, S. R. (1978). "Major Influences on Employee Attendance: A Process Model." *Journal of Applied Psychology, 63*, pp. 391–407.

―――. (1984). "Knowledge and Speculation about Absenteeism." In P. S. Goodman and R. S. Atkin (eds.), *Absenteeism: New Approaches to Understanding, Measuring, and Managing Absence*, pp. 229–275. San Francisco: Jossey-Bass.

Stephens, T. A., and Burroughs, W. A. (1978). "An Application of Operant Conditioning to Absenteeism in a Hospital Setting." *Journal of Applied Psychology, 63*, pp. 518–521.

Steward, G. V., and Larsen, J. M. (1971). "A Four-Day–Three-Day Per Week Application to a Continuous-Production Operation." *Management of Personnel Quarterly, 10*(4), pp. 3–20.

Swart, J. C. (August 1988). "Corporate Smoking Policies: Today and Tomorrow." *Personnel, 65*, pp. 61–66.

Tasto, D. L., and Colligan, M. J. (1977). *Shiftwork Practices in the United States* (DHEW Publication No. (NIOSH) 77-148). Washington, D.C.: U.S. Government Printing Office.

Taylor, F. W. (1911). *The Principles of Scientific Management.* New York: Norton.

Taylor, P. J. (1967). "Shift and Day Work: A Comparison of Sickness Absence, Lateness, and Other Absence Behaviour at an Oil Refinery from 1962 to 1965." *British Journal of Industrial Medicine, 24,* pp. 93–101.

Taylor, P. J., Pocock, S. J., and Sergean, R. (1972). "Absenteeism of Shift and Day Workers: A Study of Six Types of Shift System in 29 Organizations." *British Journal of Industrial Medicine, 29,* pp. 208–213.

Tellenback, S., Brenner, S., and Lofgren, H. (1983). "Teacher Stress: Exploratory Model Building." *Journal of Occupational Psychology, 56,* pp. 19–33.

Terborg, J. R. (1986). "Health Promotion at the Worksite: A Research Challenge for Personnel and Human Resources Management." In K. M. Rowland and G. R. Ferris (eds.), *Research in Personnel and Human Resources Management,* Vol. 4, pp. 225–267. Greenwich, CT: JAI Press.

Terborg, J. R., Lee, T. W., Smith, F. J., Davis, G. A., and Turbin, M. S. (1982). "Extension of the Schmidt and Hunter Validity Generalization Procedure to the Prediction of Absenteeism Behavior from Knowledge of Job Satisfaction and Organizational Commitment." *Journal of Applied Psychology, 67,* pp. 440–449.

Terborg, J. R., and others. (1980). *A Multivariate Investigation of Employee Absenteeism.* Technical Report No. 80–5. Houston: University of Houston.

Thiis-Evensen, E. (1958). "Shift Work and Health." *Industrial Medicine and Surgery, 27,* pp. 493–497.

Tjersland, T. (December 1972). *Changing Worker Behavior.* New York: American Telephone and Telegraph Company, Manpower Laboratory.

Trice, H. M., and Roman, P. M. (1972). *Spirits and Demons at Work.* Ithaca, N.Y.: New York State School of Industrial and Labor Relations.

Trost, C. (March 18, 1988). "Creative Child-Care Programs Aid Employees Who Work Odd Hours." *Wall Street Journal*, p. 29.

U.S. Department of Health, Education, and Welfare (1973). *Work in America: Report of a Special Task Force to the Secretary of Health, Education, and Welfare.* Cambridge, Mass.: MIT Press.

U.S. Public Health Service (1979). *Smoking and Health: A Report of the Surgeon-General* (DHEW Pub. No. PHS 79-50066). Washington, D.C.: U.S. Public Health Service.

"Van Pooling Progress Continues." (October 1983). *Dun's Business Month, 122*(4), p. 129.

Vroom, V. (1964). *Work and Motivation.* New York: Wiley.

Walker, J., and de la Mare, G. (1971). "Absence from Work in Relation to Length and Distribution of Shift Hours." *British Journal of Industrial Medicine, 28,* pp. 36–44.

Wallin, J. A., and Johnson, R. D. (1976). "The Positive Reinforcement Approach to Controlling Absenteeism." *Personnel Journal, 55,* pp. 390–392.

Walsh, D. C. (1984). "Corporate Smoking Policies; A Review and an Analysis." *Journal of Occupational Medicine, 26,* pp. 17–22.

Walters, R. W. (1982). "The Citibank Project: Improving Productivity through Work Redesign." In R. Zager and M. P. Rosow (eds.). *The Innovative Organization,* pp. 109–124. New York: Pergamon Press.

Walton, R. E. (1972). "How to Counter Alienation in the Plant." *Harvard Business Review, 50*(4), pp. 70–81.

Wanous, J. P. (1975). "Tell It Like It Is at Realistic Job Previews." *Personnel, 52*(4), pp. 50–60.

———. (1980). *Organizational Entry: Recruitment, Selection, and Socialization of Newcomers.* Reading, Mass.: Addison-Wesley.

———. (1989). "Installing a Realistic Job Preview: Ten Tough Choices." *Personnel Psychology, 42,* pp. 117–134.

Watson, C. J. (1981). "An Evaluation of Some Aspects of the Steers and Rhodes Model of Employee Attendance." *Journal of Applied Psychology, 66*, pp. 385–389.

Weiss, W. L. (1981). "Can You Afford to Hire Smokers?" *Personnel Administrator, 26*(5), pp. 71–78.

Wexley, K. N., and Nemeroff, W. F. (1975). "Effectiveness of Positive Reinforcement and Goal Setting as Methods of Management Development." *Journal of Applied Psychology, 60*, pp. 446–450.

Wheeler, K. E. (1972). "Impact of the Rearranged Workweek on Motivation and Productivity." Paper presented at the Conference on Productivity and the Four-Day Workweek, Society for Humanistic Management, Annapolis, Md.

White, J. R., and Froeb, H. F. (1980). "Small Airways Dysfunction in Nonsmokers Chronically Exposed to Tobacco Smoke." *The New England Journal of Medicine, 302*, pp. 720–723.

Winkler, D. R. (1980). "The Effects of Sick-Leave Policy on Teacher Absenteeism." *Industrial and Labor Relations Review, 33*, pp. 232–239.

Wolfe, R. A., Ulrich, D. O., and Parker, D. F. (1987). "Employee Health Management Programs: Review, Critique, and Research Agenda." *Journal of Management, 13*(4), pp. 603–615.

Woodsides, K. T. (1980). "Yes, Management, Your Medical Department Can Affect the 'Bottom Line.'" *Journal of Occupational Medicine, 22*(4), pp. 232–234.

Woska, W. J. (January 1972). "Sick Leave Incentive Plans – A Benefit to Consider." *Public Personnel Review, 33*, pp. 21–24.

Wyatt, S., and Marriott, R. (1953). "Night Work and Shift Changes." *British Journal of Industrial Medicine, 10*, pp. 164–172.

Yankelovich, D. (August 16, 1979). "We Need New Motivational Tools." *Industry Week.*

Youngblood, S. A. (1984). "Work, Nonwork, and Withdrawal." *Journal of Applied Psychology, 69*, pp. 106–117.

Author Index

199

Subject Index

Absence
    categories, 18, 19
    meaning of, 11, 12
    measurement of, 12, 13
    policies, 104
    reduction, 65, 66
"absence bank", 70
Absence behavior, 11
    charting of, 94
Absence control policies, 12, 58, 59, 164
    attendance reward programs, 70–72
    behavior identification, 92
    designing of, 65–98
    employee bonuses, 72–77
    evaluation of, 97, 98
    implementation of, 92–98
    intervention strategies, 96, 97
    mixed consequence systems, 89–92
    operant conditioning, 67–70
    reinforcement programs, 81–89
Absence control programs
    functional analysis, 94, 96
Absence control systems, 165
Absence culture, 40, 41, 54, 58, 60, 63
    salience in, 56
    trust in, 56
Absence data, 31, 94
    methods of gathering, 16, 18
Absence history, 102
    advantages in using, 103
    reference checks, 103
Absence metrics,

types of measures used, 19, 21–25
Absences
    paid and unpaid, 25, 28
Absenteeism
    assessment, 15–31
    causes, 33–63
    consequences, 7–11
    costs, 6
    determinants, 6, 7
    diagnostic model, 55–63
    early approaches to study of, 33–43
    extent of, 2–6
    future agenda for research,
      166–169
    initial propositions of, 2–11
    problem of, 1
    problems in study of, 11–14
    reasons for measuring, 15–18
    summary, 163–169
Accidents
    effect on attendance, 61
Adjacency measures, 24
Adjustment to work models, 34–41
Advertising managers
    bonus program for, 74
After-school programs, 155
Age
    absenteeism, 47, 48, 50, 102–103
    differences in absence rates, 5
Alcohol abuse, 136, 138, 139
American Society of Personnel Administration (ASPA), 70, 72, 75, 85